STEP INSIDE

THE UNFILTERED TRUTH ABOUT LISTING AND SELLING YOUR HOME

BY

DAVID ORSO, MBA

Published by CreateSpace Independent Publishing Platform
www.davidorso.com

ISBN:1491283807
ISBN 13:9781491283806

Library of Congress Control Number:2013922852
CreateSpace Independent Publishing Platform
North Charleston, South Carolina

This book is dedicated to my loving wife, Dawn Orso. Your strength, determination and strong will continue to amaze me every day. You always give 110% to everything you do.

In honor of my wife:

100% of
the Proceeds From the Sale of This Book
Benefit the Anne Arundel Medical Center

aahs.org

ACKNOWLEDGMENTS

Taking on a project like this requires a massive amount of support, encouragement, and commitment. My professional life is a direct result of the love and support I receive from my family. My wife, Dawn, is an amazing cheerleader for my success and has been through the good times and the bad times of turbulent real estate markets. She knows I am working in my field of passion and lets me work long hours serving my clients. I am blessed to have a partner to support and encourage me to go way above the call of duty, daily. My parents have been an incredible inspiration for me in this book's preparation. My mother and father have read and edited many versions and chapters and had the honesty to challenge content, concepts, and tone. I am not sure I would have ever aspired to write a book if they hadn't taught me the value of reaching for goals and working tirelessly to achieve them. Ultimately, my greatest source of inspiration is my children: Amelia, Olivia, and Max. My most cherished gifts in the world give me endless optimism and a reason to lead a life of integrity. My greatest aspiration in life is to be a role model for them. Amelia, Olivia, and Max, I love you.

In the months leading up to the release of this book, there is one person who revised content regularly. Kristy Stephens, you are the best at what you do, and my respect for you is boundless. Thank you for being so thorough with our edits and so committed to learning the topic's content toward making this the best book it could possibly be! This dream would not have been fulfilled without you. Thank you so very much.

Last but not least, I would like to thank the hundreds of clients who have trusted me with the management of their real estate needs. Your belief in me and trust in my professional capabilities, integrity, and experience are fuel for what I do every day. Each of you has a unique story, and being a part of your life has meant so much to me. I cherish our relationships and look forward to serving you again in the future. Thank you so much for your support!

CONTENTS

INTRODUCTION

I love real estate. It is that simple. I love my job, and I love working to address my clients' real estate needs. It is an honor and incredible responsibility to help individuals manage the largest asset they may ever own. I take my fiduciary obligation seriously and hope this book helps spread the word about the RIGHT way to sell real estate and that it leads you in the direction of finding a competent professional. The home-selling process has gotten a bit glamorized by the reality television syndrome which shows agents throwing extraordinary parties and contractors making major renovations for under $1,000. Television is far from reality. Selling your property in the real world requires knowledge, market insight, a game plan, and, most importantly, an agent with a professional skill set. This book is focused on the listing process and on helping you find and hire the best agent to help sell your home.

One of the neat things about my profession is that it affects nearly everyone. Shelter is a primary need. From renting a college house with friends or finding your first apartment, to buying a family home or downsizing in your empty-nester years, all have an experience with housing during their lives. Personal stories are plentiful, and it is an honor to be a part of so many people's lives as they decide to buy and sell real estate.

Throughout this book, I will be brutally honest in presenting the characteristics of competent professionals so that you, the homeowner, can find the good ones! It is my hope that this book offers a great deal of value in preparation for hiring the appropriate agent to represent you and ultimately sell your home.

By reading this book, you are already taking a step in the right direction! So please join me and "step inside"…

SECTION I

REAL ESTATE REAL TALK

CHAPTER 1

WHY 5 PERCENT OF AGENTS SELL 95 PERCENT OF THE REAL ESTATE

It has been said that 5 percent of the agents sell 95 percent of the real estate. Think about that for a second. For every one hundred homes that are sold, five agents sold ninety-five of them. In most markets, this statistic is consistently accurate. Even if it isn't exactly 5 percent selling 95 percent, it is darn close. Ever wonder why that happens?

Here is something you should be aware of: it is embarrassingly easy to become a real estate agent. The lack of entry barriers into this very important field is extremely frustrating to me. It makes me sick to think a family member or friend might put a large investment in the hands of a "real estate agent" whose only requirements for licensure were taking prelicensing courses, passing state and national exams, and signing on with a brokerage. In my area, the prelicense course is only sixty hours. That isn't much time to master the field, including all the national and state laws. Your home may be your largest asset, so protect it!

This profession requires an ability to solve complex issues with a wide range of implications. Hire a professional with extensive knowledge, training, experience, a network of professionals, and a proven track record of success. If you decide to work with a "beginning" agent, make sure he or she has partnered with a more seasoned agent and is consulting with that person throughout the entire process.

The bottom line is that experience is important in this field as opposed to just finding an agent out of convenience or friendship. So how do you find the 5 percent or so agents doing nearly all the business, and does that mean they are the best?

Finding the agents who are doing the business

When you interview an agent, it is very important to ask him questions that require factual data about his performance. It is fair to ask for a report of the top ten agents in your county for the last twelve months. If he refuses to provide this data, there may be a reason, like he isn't in the top ten! It is also likely that an agent will sidestep the question with data about his office being really great. Please keep in mind that you are not hiring an office. You are hiring a personal representative. In addition, most agents are not employees of offices. They are 1099 independent contractors, so the idea of hiring a "firm" is just inaccurate.

Chapter 7 of this book is dedicated to the "twenty-one questions every seller should ask his or her agent" before hiring one. If you do a good job sticking to the questions and demanding substantive answers, you will definitely find an agent with a track record worthy of being hired to represent you in the sale of your home.

Does being a top performer mean he or she is the best agent for the job?

Being in the top five percent in an area is exactly that. Those individuals are tops in their field, and they should know the market activity extremely well because they are dealing regularly with buyers and sellers. These individuals are typically full-time professionals with an inside track on what is happening in the market. Why would you want to deal with someone who isn't the best in his or her field? Seriously, think about that question: Why in the world would you deal with someone who isn't the best in his or her field?

Here is the best part of this whole discussion: the good, experienced agents cost the same as the unqualified agents! That's right: you can hire the Donald Trump of real estate to represent you for the same price as an inexperienced person who got his license yesterday. What an amazing benefit! The industry norm is about 3 percent commission, regardless of experience.

It is also important to find someone who is well suited to your personality. Just because someone is number one does not mean his style or personality is a good match. Take time to make sure you like being with the agent and that you trust his advice. For example, let's say there is an agent who sells a lot of homes but has a horrible reputation for returning phone calls. If service and responsiveness are important to you, then this agent might not be a good fit.

A track record of success is likely the best indicator of future performance. It is important to select an agent who is top in his field, has tremendous statistics, and also comes highly recommended.

KEY POINTS FROM CHAPTER 1:

1. Ask agents for their performance data and hire a star agent.

2. Interview top agents and find a good personality match.

3. Ask for references. A good agent should be able to provide at least ten references from recent sales.

CHAPTER 2

FOLLOW THE CLUES

Great marketers are like detectives searching for data and trends because they know they leave clues. Strategic marketers use research and studies to formulate marketing plans that are in sync with consumer behaviors. Competently listing a home for sale requires that same keen attention to research trends and an acute awareness of home-buyer behaviors.

It may feel like you are the only one in the world selling your home, but the truth is millions of families sell each year, and the data leaves clues. The National Association of REALTORS® is a tremendous resource for our industry and is the leading research body about consumer trends in residential real estate. Their statistical findings create a road map for finding buyers. Let's review some of the data from the *Profile of Home Buyers and Sellers 2012* and piece it together to formulate an actual game plan for selling in today's world.

Facts about Home Buyers

Fact 1:   39 percent of sales are first-time home buyers

Fact 2:   The typical buyer is forty-two years old

Fact 3:   Median household income $78,600

Fact 4:   65 percent of buyers are married

Fact 5:   Top three factors for home bought: quality of neighborhood, convenience to job, and overall affordability

Interpretation:

It is clear from the studies that homeownership is still viewed as a favorable investment and consumer confidence remains strong for residential housing. In other words, the American dream of owning a home is alive and well.

As a seller of a home, the facts show us that featuring the community and location of the home is key in the decision-making process for buyers. On the flip side, if your home is not in a community or convenient to major highways, this could be an issue. The old adage "location, location, location" rings true. Since you can't change the location of your home, your agent may have to emphasize other key selling features of your home.

Facts about the Home Search Process

Fact 1: 90 percent of buyers used the Internet to search for homes

Fact 2: 96 percent of buyers under the age of forty-four used the   Internet to search for homes

Fact 3: The typical buyer searched for twelve weeks and previewed ten homes before writing an offer

Fact 4: 87 percent found their real estate agent to be a useful source of information during the home-buying process

Fact 5: 89 percent of buyers purchased their home with the assistance of a real estate agent

Interpretation:

The real estate agent continues to be the number one source for brokering a transaction while the consumer clearly uses the Internet as the primary source for gathering information. That means that today's seller has a clear path to selling his or her home: look amazing online and find a competent agent.

The Internet is being used to sort homes for buyers. Open houses, brochures, postcards, and other forms of marketing are somewhat archaic in today's real estate world. Buyers are gathering important information online before they ever go through a home. As a home seller this is a HUGE clue! In the olden days, tactics like open houses and postcards were necessary because buyers could not see the home without them. Now, buyers simply go online to preview pictures and take virtual tours along with researching your price compared to similar homes that have sold.

The inception of the Internet has changed the game so quickly that I still hear questions like, "Are you going to hold an open house?" Houses are now open 24-7, and buyers clearly are choosing to preview homes online as opposed to in person. It is astonishing that buyers preview, on average, only ten homes in person before buying. They are compressing their searches by previewing many homes online and then only their favorite ones on site.

As a seller, if you aren't getting on-site showings, then your home is most likely being rejected online. This could be due to a poor online presentation of your home or the list price being off the mark.

Facts about Financing

Fact 1: 87 percent of buyers borrowed money to buy a home

Fact 2: 91 percent was the average loan to value for amount borrowed

Fact 3: 65 percent of buyers used savings for their down payment, and 25 percent used proceeds from sale of their home

Fact 4: 78 percent of buyers made sacrifices during the buying process such as cutting spending on luxury items, entertainment, and clothes

Fact 5: 78 percent of buyers felt that buying a home was a good financial investment

Interpretation:

Even after the housing crisis our country experienced recently, the vast majority of buyers felt that home buying was a good investment.

One interesting trend since the housing bubble burst is that buyers are using savings to buy a home and not just the proceeds from selling a home. It is refreshing to see that trend and it should contribute to long-term solvency of our housing market. In the same breath, buyers are making sacrifices during the home-buying process in anticipation of expenses.

The most telling statistic, though, is that 87 percent of buyers obtained a mortgage to buy a home. As a seller, this has implications such as an appraisal and possibly repair items required by the lender. My advice would be to make sure the buyer of your home is using a reputable lender and that you complete necessary repairs before listing.

Facts about Home Sellers

Fact 1: Nine years is the average amount of time sellers stay in a home

Fact 2: 88 percent of sellers used a real estate agent

Fact 3: 40 percent of sellers offered incentives

Fact 4: 46 percent of sellers traded up to a larger and higher priced home

Fact 5: Nineteen miles is the average distance between home sold and home purchased

Interpretation:

Sellers aren't moving very far and don't seem to stay in a home as long as one may think. As families grow, so do the needs for a larger home. Again, the real estate agent is controlling the sale on the listing side just as we found out on the buying side. This fact is very important because two agents will definitely be able to validate the appropriate positioning of a home in the market. Even if your listing agent agrees to list your home for sale at the wrong price, the buyer's agent will not permit it to sell at that price.

If the average stay in a home is less than ten years, it would also be prudent to make sure any and all renovations are closely reviewed and the impact on sales price is fully understood. I commonly hear home sellers telling me how much something cost as if they think they will financially recoup the full cost of their selections.

Facts about Home Sales:

Fact 1: Eleven weeks is the average amount of time to sell

Fact 2: 95 percent is the average sales price to list price

Fact 3: 60 percent of home sellers reduced their asking price

Fact 4: $20,000 was the average equity earned in selling the home

Interpretation:

Listing your home isn't enough. To really get the home sold, it takes flexibility, expert salesmanship, and a willingness to adjust pricing. The really good news about selling your home is that it happens pretty quickly if you do a good job preparing the home for sale, price it right, make it look spectacular online, and make it accessible for buyers to preview.

KEY POINTS FROM CHAPTER 2:

1. Review data very closely with your agent before listing.

2. Make sure you have a strong online presence.

3. Make sure you don't overprice.

4. If you don't get on-site showings right away, something is likely wrong. Make a quick adjustment.

CHAPTER 3

THE FIFTEEN BIGGEST MYTHS IN LISTING REAL ESTATE

When selling your home, it is important to understand the difference between real estate fact and fiction. Your home is most likely your most valuable and expensive asset. The following are fifteen myths I have come across during my years in the industry.

Myth 1:
"THE LISTING AGREEMENT IS FOR ONE YEAR"

I receive calls frequently from frustrated home sellers who have had their home on the market and want to change agents. They review their listing agreement and realize they signed a one-year agreement. Why was it for one year? Is that the law? No! A listing agreement's term and all of the conditions are 100 percent negotiable and flexible.

My listing agreement has a cancellation clause because I am confident my sellers will be extremely pleased with their experience. Why would anyone need a one-year listing agreement? If it takes a year to sell your home, there is a problem! If there is a problem, then shouldn't you be able to cancel the agreement? However, some agents will ask you to sign a one-year listing agreement. They may tell you it is their office's policy. If it is their office's policy, then I recommend you interview a new agent with flexible terms and a performance guarantee.

Here are the terms I think are 100 percent fair for a listing agreement:

1. Cancel-at-any-time policy, with one-day notice.

2. If the seller decides to take his or her home off the market prematurely, then the seller should reimburse the agent for reasonable costs incurred.

Myth 2:
"BOTH SIDES OF THE DEAL"

It is illegal for an agent to work both sides of a transaction. The agent listing your home works for you and cannot also work for the buyer. The agency law is very specific, but some agents break the law.

More than ever this is becoming an issue because home buyers have access to the listings through the Internet and call the listing agents directly. The listing agents are obviously excited because they think they'll make the full commission instead of half the commission. So they show the home to the potential buyers themselves. This is legitimate IF and ONLY IF the agents have the buyers sign an agency agreement acknowledging they work for the sellers. Most buyers don't understand this and should be informed.

Be sure your agent specifies how he or she would handle this type of situation and demand that any and all buyers have their own representation. It is unethical and not acting in the sellers' best interests for an agent to work "both sides."

Myth 3:
"PRINT ADVERTISING IN NEWSPAPERS OR MAGAZINES IS EFFECTIVE"

Home sellers love to see advertising for their home, and there is an impulse reaction to ask the agent if their home will be in the newspaper. The Internet has overwhelmed and outperformed print advertising. According to the National Association of REALTORS®' 2012 *Profile of Home Buyers and Sellers*, 92 percent of home buyers used the Internet in their search. Off-line, 88 percent of buyers turn to a real estate agent to assist them with their search. Other off-line channels such as newspaper advertisements and home magazines play a minimal role in buyers' research and decision-making process. In fact, 73 percent of buyers rarely or never use print advertising. Less than 2 percent of respondents in the National Association of

REALTORS® survey said they found their home in a print publication.

Three reasons agents still advertise listings in the newspaper are:

1. A seller demands newspaper advertisements, and the listing agent is scared to tell them the truth.

2. The newspaper is a way for an agent to advertise themselves by putting his or her own face in the paper.

3. The agent hasn't caught up with the times or research.

If an agent suggests only print media or shows you different ads he has run recently, then you should consider another agent. He is leading you down an unwise path. Don't be fooled by the shiny object! It looks great and we all love to see our home in the paper, but you really do want to sell your home, right? If you want to sell your home, follow the clues and go where the buyers are looking!

Myth 4:
"SELLERS DETERMINE THE LISTING PRICE"

Some agents are so desperate to get the listing agreement signed that they will let you name the starting price.

These agents suggest that the price doesn't matter: just sign the agreement and the agent is happy. Then the agent comes to you thirty days later and asks for a price reduction. Like most sellers, you will likely get upset, not because it isn't the right thing to do, but because you were not advised correctly up front. You may feel as if you were conned.

The value of your home should be discussed and deliberated at length. An experienced agent will discuss with you a pricing strategy that includes a reasonable starting price and a timeline for lowering the price if it hasn't sold.

Some agents will grossly misrepresent the value of your home just to get the listing. On many occasions, I have competed for a listing with other agents who have given the sellers a price much higher than the accurate one. Every seller dreams of getting big money for her home, but it should not be the reason you select an agent.

If an agent tells you a price for your home that you feel is too high because "he thinks he can get it," or if an agent tells you a price that seems too low and is unable to back it up with data, consider interviewing other agents.

A true professional will help educate you about pricing your home and the consequences of over- or underpricing. A true professional will not allow you to do the wrong thing but will lead you in the right direction. If you are unwilling to take the professional agent's fact-based counsel, the agent should turn down your listing so that she is not a part of a situation doomed to fail.

Myth 5:
"I HAVE A BUYER FOR YOUR HOME"

All sellers are desperate to hear, "I have a buyer for your home!" Some agents will tell a seller just that, despite the truth. If your listing agent tells you she has a buyer, ask her who she is working for—you or the buyer. Watch how quickly that buyer of hers isn't going to be buying or how quickly that buyer found another home. It is an extremely unfair sales tactic to get you excited!

Another common tactic by agents is to send out a letter to a neighborhood stating they have buyers looking to buy in the area. Wow, that is an amazing proposition: selling your home without the hassles or fees of an agent is a compelling pitch. But the reality is that the agent doesn't have a buyer; the agent is fishing for a listing. Your response to the marketing letter identifies you as a seller to the agent. Before you know it, you are sitting through a listing presentation instead of being presented with a buyer.

The law of agency in real estate states that an agent can work for only one party. If an agent has a buyer, then he is the buyer's agent, plain and simple. The fact that an agent is bragging to a seller about having a buyer shows gross negligence and disregard for any knowledge of the law.

To get maximum value for your home, it is best to expose it to the largest number of potential buyers possible. Showing the home to the apparent phantom buyer is foolish if you haven't tested the home on a fair market.

Myth 6:
"THE NEIGHBORHOOD SPECIALIST"

This is one of the most troubling myths because it so commonly used. Agents who live in a neighborhood will act and say things like they "own" a specific neighborhood. How in the world does where you live affect your ability to prepare, market, and negotiate a property? It has no bearing on an agent's skill set; it is just her address.

There is a perception that the agent living in the community knows the neighborhood better or will fight harder because he lives there. Knowing the neighborhood and its features is something a seller should discuss with the listing agent before the home goes on the market. An effective marketing plan should expose all the unique factors a neighborhood has to offer. The fact that someone lives in the community is irrelevant. Your agent should become very knowledgeable about the neighborhood.

Ask for the previous twelve months of sales statistics to see if anyone really dominates your neighborhood. My bet is there are several agents selling homes and representing buyers in your neighborhood.

Myth 7:
"THE NUMBER ONE AGENT"

If you read the advertisements in the weekend paper, you would be fascinated to see that there are probably about seven number one agents in your local area. How is that possible? Agents are notorious for making themselves number one at something: number one in their office, number one in their neighborhood, number one in their county, number one for waterfront, number one for golf course homes sold, number one for townhomes, number one for fifty-five and over. You get the point: a lot of it is marketing jargon and not really an indication of anything other than agents trying to look good. If an agent says he is number one, he should be able to back it up with real data.

When listing your home, there are three statistics that really matter:

1. **Percentage of listings sold.** You should ask your agent how many listings he had in the last twenty-four months and how many actually sold.

2. **Days on Market.** You should ask your agent for a report showing how long it takes him to sell listings.

3. **Sales Price to List Price Ratio.** This is an indication of how well agents predict a sales price and how well they negotiate for their sellers. You should ask your agent for a report of his sales and review the sales price to list price ratio.

In addition to those three statistics, you should ask the agent what the market average is for your particular area.

A good agent will have his figures in order and be able to compare them to the other agents and market figures. It isn't about being number one in a small category; it is about being excellent at your trade.

Myth 8:
"THE 24-7 AGENT"

What if your doctor, accountant, or attorney handled all the administrative paperwork associated with their line of work in addition to working with you as the patient or client? Smart business professionals know that you do the tasks for which you are trained and skilled. You outsource the other tasks to those who specialize in those areas.

If real estate agents are not doing much business, they may be able to handle all the tasks associated with the job. But then they probably aren't bringing in enough business for it to qualify as a "job."

Successful real estate agents will have one or more assistants and possibly additional agents working for them to support their business. The agent may not be personally available 24-7 because they have enough business sense to hire well-qualified staff to handle specific tasks and provide superior customer service. The bottom line is that in most cases no one can do it all, and if they try, the process will eventually break down; the result will be poor service to the client.

Myth 9:
"A COMPREHENSIVE MARKETING PLAN"

Some agents do not have a marketing plan other than putting a sign in the yard and entering your listing into a multiple listing service. When pushed for a marketing plan, these agents may scramble and suggest things like open houses, brokers' open houses, print advertising, and anything else you may want to hear. However, a valid marketing plan needs to be more than just a few signs and an open house. In fact, open houses are typically more beneficial to the agent than the seller. They are a great place for the agent to gather leads, but serious and "ready" buyers are most likely already working with another agent and will request a private showing.

A true marketing plan incorporates the four *p*'s of marketing: price, promotion, product, and placement.

1. **Pricing** is the most crucial part of your marketing plan in real estate, and a genuine professional will help educate you about the complexity of a pricing strategy.

2. **Promotion** of your property is the activity an agent will do to generate interest among fellow agents and buyers.

3. **Product** is your home, and your agent should help you present it in the very best light to buyers.

4. **Placement** is the location of your home. Accentuating the features of your neighborhood, local schools, area amenities, local events, and the other nuances of a specific location are HUGE in the sales process. Most people are familiar with the old adage about the three most important things in real estate: "location, location, location."

Myth 10:
"IT ONLY TAKES ONE BUYER"

Agents will try to make sellers feel good about not getting showings by saying, "It only takes one buyer." But the truth is, if you are not getting showings, buyers have rejected the product you are offering for sale.

If your home isn't selling, then it probably doesn't look like it is worth its list price. Make major adjustments to the home's conditions, get better photographs, or lower the price, and I bet you start getting showings that might help you find the "one buyer." Let go of false hope and deal with the realities of selling.

In my local market, roughly 50 percent of homes do not sell. This incredibly scary fact is not cured by saying things like, "It only takes one buyer." Last year, 50 percent of sellers never found the one buyer. Hire an agent who tells the truth. Telling the truth means telling you exactly what you need to hear based on facts, data, and logic, not what you want to hear by using clichés.

Myth 11:
"AGENTS HAVE AN ONLINE STRATEGY"

The truth is that the real estate industry is typically "behind the times" when it comes to technology. The Internet is complex, and some agents do not have the technical knowledge and skills needed, the time to learn it, or the staff to assist with it. However, online is where the buyers are, so it needs to be understood to effectively market a home for sale.

A good agent should be able to demonstrate to you the use of technology with specific properties and how she responds to online inquires. One of the keys to online marketing is having a system to respond nearly immediately to customer inquiries.

Many brokerages have successfully managed to negotiate deals with the larger website companies such as Zillow.com, Trulia.com, realtor.com, and homes.com. These sites drive most of the online traffic. However, a web inquiry (a lead) needs to be responded to very quickly. So be certain to ask your agent how he handles web leads. Look for a specific plan of action.

Myth 12:
"AGENTS ARE TOUGH NEGOTIATORS AND WANT THE BEST DEAL FOR YOU"

This will be discussed in chapter 6 when identifying the four roles of an agent. Most agents will tell you they are tough negotiators, and you probably expect an agent to have that skill. While some agents may be really good negotiators, it is important to consider an agent's motivation level. According to the National Association of REALTORS®' *Member Profile 2013*, the median gross income of REALTORS® was $43,500 in 2012. This is the amount earned BEFORE expenses, which typically run around 50 percent. In my local market, netting $21,750 a year is not a good wage. How tough do you really think a low-earning agent will be when it comes to negotiating a deal for you? Do you think he'll just want to get the deal done and get paid? Unfortunately, in many cases, that is what happens.

A successful agent will be able to provide good counsel to you because he has a clear head and is not worried about his next paycheck. He has enough business and doesn't have the monetary pressures of an agent doing very little business. A good negotiator will always try to get you the best possible deal and not settle for just an easy "good enough."

Choosing a low-performing agent could cost you thousands and thousands of dollars. The agent's ability to negotiate on your behalf is his most significant value.

Myth 13:
"YOU WON'T GET YOUR MONEY BACK ON REPAIRS"

During the past few years, the economy has been very tight and most sellers were not profiting on their home sales. Therefore, they were reluctant to put any money into making repairs or staging (preparing a home to increase its overall appeal). Some agents will go along with the objections about paint and carpet or other necessary staging items. Good agents know that you will most likely need to make repairs and improve the condition of a home to sell it. It can be challenging to convince a homeowner to make the necessary improvements, but it is the job of the agent to provide accurate counsel.

If an agent lets you dismiss, without a good reason, stained carpets, water leaks, obnoxious paint colors, and other mechanical or cosmetic issues, he should not be your representative. I strongly recommend all sellers visit a model home of a reputable local homebuilder before listing their home for sale. The model homes are impeccably clean and free of debris and clutter. This is how your home should look; if not, you will be penalized severely in your price.

Think about selling a car. Would you get it washed and detailed? Of course you would, and you should do the same for your home before you list it.

Myth 14:
"AGENTS JUST KNOW THE MARKET"

Knowing the state of the market is the result of being able to analyze trends supported by data and facts. Your agent should bring ample data to the conversation about what is happening in your neighborhood, your price point, your home style, school quality, etc.

The old detective's saying, "Just the facts, ma'am, just the facts," is especially true here. Don't believe the agent who talks and talks and talks. Believe the data and statistics. A good agent will bring accurate market data that is relevant *and* easy to understand. This data is very important and should be followed closely. Occasionally, I have seen agents do a great job with the data, but the client disagrees anyway. When this happens, the agent needs to warn the client that the market is harsh and will reject their emotion.

Myth 15:
"LIST WITH 'THE' BROKERAGE IN YOUR AREA"

Some brokerages love to act like they sell all the homes and even sell them before they are listed. It sounds good and creates an elitist mentality among their agents. A real estate sales office is just a physical location with a bunch of desks, computers, and offices. The brokerage that an agent works for is only as good as the services it provides to the agent. Almost all agents are 1099 independent contractors who work under a broker. For you, the agent is more important than the broker because the agent is your representative. Cool brokerages and office locations do not sell homes. What sells a home is a well-executed plan by a well-trained listing agent.

If an agent tells you her office dominates an area, ask her for a breakdown of all home sales in your county in the last twelve months. If you really want to throw her off, ask how many of the agents in her brokerage office sold less than ten homes last year. Brokerages love to act like having a lot of agents is a good thing. Having a prime retail location with a lot of nonproducing agents is not a good thing! Stick to the facts and data about the agent and avoid the "brokerage propaganda" trap.

In the end, if an agent is presenting a tremendous amount of information about his brokerage, then he is likely insecure about his own capabilities. The individual agent is your representative; measure the specific individual.

KEY POINTS FROM CHAPTER 3:

1. Let statistics do the talking.

2. Ask a lot of questions.

3. Be an educated seller.

CHAPTER 4

A HOME IS WORTH WHATEVER A BUYER IS WILLING TO PAY

The title of this chapter is a concept that may be hard to grasp. The reason: Your home is most likely very special to you, and you may feel that it is unique in some way compared to the others in your area. The truth about selling a home is that the buyer is in control and determines the value. As the homeowner, you can name an asking price (after a discussion with your agent, of course!), but the buyers will ultimately determine the value.

One of the keys to selling your home is to remove the emotional attachment. Once you decide to put your home on the market, it becomes a commodity on the open market. I know on a personal level the emotional battle between wanting to sell your home and not wanting to leave memories behind. Furthermore, you could have poured your blood, sweat, and tears into renovating the home at some point. All those emotions, memories, and days of hard work are irrelevant to buyers when they are evaluating your home in comparison to others on the market.

THE HOUSE-HUNTING PROCESS

Let's think about this from the perspective of the modern-day buyer. We have already established that buyers are using the Internet to look at homes and compare them online before visiting the property. Buyers are comparing your home to all the other homes in the same price range. Real estate websites also give an indication of value to help buyers understand if the pricing is accurate or not.

Buyers do a majority of their research and review before ever walking through your front door. To get them in the door, your home needs to match or be better than the other homes in the same price point. If your home is overpriced or appears inferior, you will not get on-site showings and ultimately not get offers. Frustrated sellers will frequently say two things: 1) "Why aren't we getting any showings?" or 2) "Just bring me an offer." If you review the process that buyers follow in their search, you will quickly realize that your home is not making the cut and is losing to other homes that buyers deem to be a fair value.

How buyers find a home and their behavioral patterns are overwhelmingly consistent. Buyers look online, drive by homes that look good online, and THEN go preview the home (Figure 1).

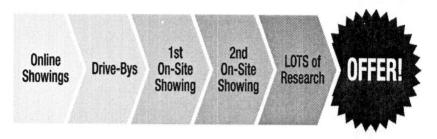

Figure 1: A depiction of how the house-hunting process typically works.

FACTORS THAT AFFECT THE VALUE OF YOUR HOME

As an agent, when it comes time to review the pricing strategy for a home, I look at several factors:

1. **Market Conditions**

   Pricing a home to sell is data-driven in the research and preparation, but it is not precise because frequently changing market conditions affect the sale of residential property. Reviewing the market conditions is a detailed process that takes into consideration factors such as current financing terms available to borrowers, buyer demand for the specified home type, local economy, supply and demand of inventory, and recent sales. A professional real estate agent will have all of this information neatly packaged to present and help you understand the local market.

Sometimes, when inventory is low, a new buyer comes to town and needs to buy quickly. The price of the home will be rewarded by the urgency. It makes perfect sense to list a home a little bit higher if your professional can justify a limited supply of homes or a market condition driving the prices up.

In my opinion, the elasticity of the market value prediction is no greater than 5 percent. If I think a home's market value is $500,000, then I believe the highest reasonable original list price would be $525,000. If the home is not getting showings and not getting offers, then the original list price was wrong and needs to be adjusted quickly.

2. **Your Motivation Level**

If you are highly motivated and need to sell quickly, obviously the price would need to reflect the need for a rapid offer. On the other hand, if you are not in a rush, the pricing strategy may reflect a higher starting price. Motivation level should always be gauged by the date you have to move. Having a date is a key ingredient to counseling you through a pricing strategy.

3. **Community Features**

Community features are critically important to review in comparison to other homes. In my local market, school districts vary greatly, and the same style and quality home may be worth $100,000 more for being in a better school district. Neighborhood amenities could include water access, community ball fields, playgrounds, summer camps, number of homes, style of homes, lot sizes, proximity to major highways and shopping, and other elements that make the community unique and enjoyable.

4. **Property Features**
   Sellers either love or hate to show agents their home. Some are very proud of their renovations and maintenance, whereas others are rather ashamed and scared to expose years of deferred maintenance and clutter buildup. The varying degrees of upkeep certainly create a spectrum of market value. Buyers may pay for a specific neighborhood, but they will not pay a premium for a fixer-upper. The best solution for gauging how your home may compare to the competition is to go with your agent and preview similar homes on the market. Be honest and fair about the condition, updates, and "showability" of your home.

5. **Exposure to the Market**
   The prelisting consultation and marketing delivered by a professional agent can make or break the sale. If you have not been counseled by a professional and your home is not being presented to the market professionally by your agent, then you will suffer. If homes simply sold themselves, I would need to find new employment. The agent's professional advice matters. His or her ability to know

how to present your home in a favorable and appropriate marketplace position equates to dollars in your pocket.

FACTORS THAT DO NOT AFFECT THE VALUE OF YOUR HOME

When it comes to pricing your home to sell, the following factors do not affect the listing price or the value of your home:

1. **Original Purchase Price**
    From 2006 to 2008, the market began a free fall and values were down 20 to 30 percent in most areas. In the years following, the most common response to the market value discussion involved how much the homeowner had paid for the home. It simply has no bearing on your home's market value. Think about it this way: if a homeowner purchased a $500,000 home for $1,000 from their grandparents' estate, should the new buyer pay only $1,000? Of course not, the home buyer would be expected to pay market value. The original purchase price has nothing to do with the current sale price.

2. **The Amount Owed**
    Another symptom of the 2006–2008 market crash was the mortgage debt owed. This becomes a major issue for homeowners who are overextended. Unfortunately, the open market shows absolutely zero

consideration for the sellers' "need-to-get" amount. If you are upside down, be honest about it and seek legal counsel if a short sale is your only option. Other options would be to rent the home or to take a loss.

3. **Renovations Made for Personal Taste**
   Overly improved homes or renovations made to accommodate personal taste do not add value to the property. I frequently see things like steam showers, exercise rooms with mirrors, closet racks, extensive garage shelving systems, light fixtures, and other things sellers have done for the sake of personal enjoyment. These types of renovations do not add value. If you are thinking of doing major improvements, consult a local professional for his or her opinion about the amount of value that could be added based on the upgrades. Additionally, you may want to take a look at *Remodeling* magazine's "Cost vs. Value Report," which compares construction cost with resale value for popular home improvement projects in eighty-one US markets. It is available at http://www.costvsvalue.com.

4. **Neighbor's Opinions**
   The uninformed neighbor trying to preserve value for his home and the community is well intended, but not a professional. Many times, I will meet with sellers who start by saying, "The neighbors want to see me get [x amount]." I certainly wish all of their cheerleading and camaraderie made a difference. However, market value is market value, plain and simple. The

uninformed neighbor can do more harm than good when he advises against price reductions or starts talking about homes he "heard" went for a certain amount. Trust the agent you have hired and trust the process the professionally informed is following.

5. **An Outdated Appraisal**
Mortgage interest rates have been dropping precipitously for the last five years, encouraging many homeowners to obtain an appraisal to refinance. However, the value of the home provided in the appraisal is a snapshot of the market at that time, and markets change daily. The buyer will get a new appraisal that will reflect the value of the home based on the current market.

PRICE REDUCTIONS

Part of a legitimate pricing strategy discussion should include the reality of price reductions. Too many agents wait to have this discussion until the home hasn't sold and everyone is frustrated. Do you think major retailers leave inventory on the shelf at the wrong price? Of course they don't. They have software systems to advise them on supply-demand and traffic patterns to help justify lowering the prices. Real estate is no different: a true professional will help educate a seller about the natural flow of showings to offers and the appropriate time frames.

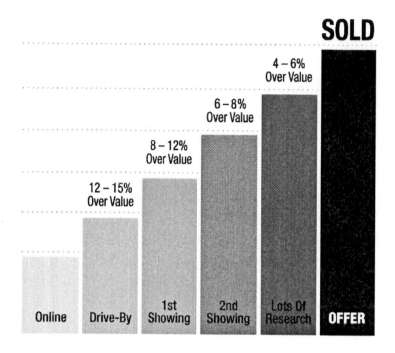

Figure 2: Step model for pricing that shows how overpricing your home can cause buyers to stop considering your home in their search process.

Figure 2 displays clearly the sales process and the ceilings some sellers will experience. This is a very powerful diagram and one of the most important points in this book. To further explain the diagram, I want to dive deeper into the possible scenarios and flow of a listing.

Scenario 1: No showings and no offers. Assuming the home is being promoted online and the seller is working with a competent agent, the home is actually getting shown online hundreds of times, and buyers are likely driving by the home on the weekend. Here is the brutal truth: the home is being shown and the home is being rejected. From my experience, if this is the point where the home is not progressing, the home is 12 to 15 percent out of position based on perceived value from active buyers.

Scenario 2: One-time showings and no offers. This is VERY common when a home has a terrific location (e.g., great schools, popular neighborhood, waterfront, etc.) and buyers are very interested in living there. Buyers want to see the home quickly, but reject the home and take it off their list just as fast. They do not request a second showing and/or do not advance in the process.

This scenario is a complete mind game for a seller. They think buyers are excited because they are showing up to preview the home. An incompetent agent will say something like, "My marketing is working because we are getting the traffic." Who in the world wants traffic? Sellers want offers!

This scenario is the most common, but the unfortunate truth is the home is likely out of position by 8 to12 percent. My professional recommendation is a quick adjustment while the buyers are interested. This phase won't last forever, and the home will become stale after about forty-five to sixty days. If an adjustment isn't made, then the sellers will wonder where all the buyers went. The honest answer? The buyers went and bought other homes.

Scenario 3: Second showings with no offers. The good news is you are close to selling your home. The bad news is you are not getting an offer. At this point in the sales process, a good agent is reaching out to the buyer's agent daily and encouraging him to write an offer. A professional agent will begin to learn about the potential buyer's situation, needs, and wants. Buyers who take the time to preview the home again are very interested and have likely brought parents, contractors, or other influencers to the home for validation of their buying decision. If these second showings don't result in an offer, the home is likely 6 to 8 percent out of position among the other homes being considered.

Scenario 4: Second showings with offers. This means you are very close to selling your home and might even have a reasonable offer in discussions. A seller should pay very close attention to the market's reaction to the home. This is the research phase of the process. Information is available and transparent to buyers in today's market. Before making an offer, buyers will crunch numbers and review data very closely with their buyer's agent and also on their own using the Internet. If the offers (written or verbal) do not meet your expectations, the home is being chosen, but it is likely out of position by 4 to 6 percent.

The difference between second showings with no offers and second showings with offers is found in the research being conducted by buyers. Buyers will not just make an offer. Buyers want to buy a home, and they don't want to play games at the risk of losing time or a home of choice. Sellers who think buyers make offers casually on homes are terribly mistaken. This isn't a forty-dollar item on eBay. This is a home, and buyers don't play games when it comes to money and their family's future residence.

Your agent should have the price reduction conversation with you before the house goes on the market. Competent advisers don't say things like, "Let's see how it goes!" A price should be reduced every thirty days if the home is not getting showings or offers. It is a tough reality for many homeowners, but it is the market reality of the home being sold.

———•———

PRICING DENIAL SYNDROME

Fair market value and pricing are very difficult to grasp, and emotion is typically the barrier to doing the right thing. The very personal nature of selling a home and the thought of being ripped off create drama in the selling process. In my years of selling homes, it is very apparent when a seller is developing "pricing denial syndrome," a phrase coined by David Knox, a leading teacher and instructor in our industry. Here is what it looks like:

Symptoms:
1. Denial: "It's not the price."

2. Minimization: "It's just a little off."

3. Blame: "You should be doing more."

4. Justification: "I need the money."

5. Bargaining: "Maybe we should keep trying for a little longer."

6. Anger: "Everyone is wrong."

7. Acceptance: "I don't care if it doesn't sell."

8. Rejection: "I will just take it off the market."

Prognosis:
You will continue to argue with the market, the market will win, and you will not sell your home.

Diagnosis:
Listen to the buyers, the buyers' agents, and your listing agent, and then adjust accordingly. If your goal is selling your home, address pricing issues or make major modifications to the home.

———◆———

AUDIENCES TO CONVINCE

The buyer isn't the only party you need to accept your price. A closer review of who needs to support and affirm a buyer's decision offers more reasons to price the home accurately from the beginning.

THE BUYER: The first person to review the listing online is typically the buyer himself. Buyers use Internet sites like Zillow to look for homes. Zillow presents a "Zestimate," which is a market analysis approach to pricing. If the list price and the Internet price don't match, the buyer is likely to move on. Additionally, buyers compare the property to other homes in the area. Convincing the buyer of market value is the first hurdle for a seller.

THE BUYER'S AGENT: The second party to be convinced of market value would be the buyer's agent. The buyer's agent will show the home and should be very knowledgeable about the other homes in the area and previous sales. If the home is priced incorrectly, the buyer's agent should immediately inform the buyers and suggest moving on to a home positioned accurately and fairly in the market. Or, if the buyers are really interested, the buyer's agent is going to suggest a lower asking price.

THE APPRAISER: If the buyer and the buyer's agent have approved the pricing and an offer has been agreed upon, an appraiser will be called to validate the price on behalf of the buyer's lender. If an appraiser cannot justify the price, then the asking price will likely be reduced, or the deal may fall through.

Fooling three parties is nearly impossible. Don't try it!

TIME IS OF THE ESSENCE

The best results typically occur the fastest when selling a home. It may be counterintuitive to the "hold out for the absolute best offer" mentality, but it is factually supported.

The table below is an analysis of my local market and the breakdown of timing and results for the homes sold.

Days on Market	Percent of Original Asking Price	Average Days to Contract	Odds of Selling
0 – 30	96.7%	13	41%
31 – 60	90.72%	45	16%
61 – 90	87.85%	76	13%
90 – 120	82.08%	248	7%

Figure 3: An analysis of my local market and the breakdown of timing and results for the homes sold.

This analysis offers significant insight about the reality of timing and pricing. There are two fascinating components to review: 1) percentage of original asking price and 2) odds of selling in relation to the days on the market.

Most sellers are incredibly fascinated to learn they will receive the most amount of money by selling quickly. The reason is simple: new inventory is more exciting than old inventory. When a buyer reviews how many days a home has been on the market, she is effectively asking if anyone else has been interested. The thought that other buyers have passed over a home for months creates doubt and fear.

The second fascinating factor is the likelihood of actually selling. Waiting for the right buyer or the right price is a myth. The odds of selling your home drop to an extremely challenging level if you have not been selected early in the process.

A quick study indicates the odds of selling don't add up to 100 percent. The reason is because a large percentage of homes fail to sell at all. The sellers just take it off the market and blame the agent, the market, or the buyers who couldn't see the value.

After reading this book, I hope you never say, "Let's price it high, and let them make offers." The facts are absolutely conclusive. Price it right and it will sell quickly for the closest amount to asking price that you will ever get. There is a consequence to not selling, and anyone who has had to carry two mortgages does not need to be reminded. The table below is a template for determining the financial impact of not selling your home quickly.

Days On Market	Odds of Selling	Mortgage Payment	Insurance	Taxes	Water	Gas & Electric	HOA	Maintenance	Declining Value	Market Value Loss	Other	TOTAL Cost of Overpricing
0 – 30												
31 – 60												
61 – 90												
90 – 120												
120 +												

Figure 4: Complete a table like this to help determine the financial impact of not selling your home quickly.

This message is repeated throughout this book: preparation is everything! If you make your home beautiful and accessible, price it right, and have a spectacular online presence, you'll be moving before you know it.

—————

KNOW YOUR NET

I always complete a net sheet for my sellers so they know exactly how much they will receive when the settlement transaction is completed. Typically, multiple net sheets are prepared to deal with the reality of different offers. If the amount of the net proceeds is unacceptable to a homeowner, we simply do not proceed, and we discuss other options. It is professionally negligent to know a price is realistically unobtainable and still list the home. There will be major aggravation for the seller and damage to the relationship between the agent and the seller. Additionally, the home may be blackballed by local agents, and the seller will be viewed as unreasonable.

SELLER'S NET SHEET

This is an estimate and is not guaranteed. Actual costs may vary based on actual closing price and terms. Consult your lender/title company for exact amounts.

Outstanding Mortgage/Lien: $ _____

ESTIMATED CLOSING COSTS

Title Company / Attorney Fees	
Local and State Taxes (1.1%)	
Federal Taxes (May be N/A)	
Listing Agent Commission	
Buyer Agent Commission	
Repair Work Costs (Staging)	
Repair Work Costs (After Inspection)	
Seller Paid Closing Cost	
Home Warranty	
Other Fees	
TOTAL Estimating Closing Costs	

ESTIMATED PROCEEDS TO SELLER AT CLOSING

	Asking Price	30–60 Day Price	60–90 Day Price	90–120 Price
Market Position				
Less Outstanding Mortgage/Liens				
Less Estimated Closing Costs				
Estimated Net Proceeds				

_____   _____
Seller   Seller

Figure 5: Sample Seller's Net Sheet

The fees included in a net proceeds sheet are:

1. Payoff of any outstanding mortgages or liens against the property.

2. Title company/attorney fees for closing the sale.

3. Real estate professional's commissions.

4. Local and state taxes for transferring real property.

5. Any federal taxes such as nonresident withholdings.

6. A small budget for home inspection items that may arise.

After reviewing the net proceeds with a seller, the reactions generally vary from "Wow, that is awesome" to "That just won't work for me." The former reaction is delightful and leads to an outstanding experience. The latter is much tougher and can lead to difficult conversations about overpricing the home as a solution to compensate for the unacceptable proceeds, as previously discussed. The idea of fooling a buyer on the value of your home is preposterous.

WHY DO AGENTS OVERPRICE HOMES?

Agents overprice homes for four reasons:

1. **LACK OF KNOWLEDGE AND EXPERIENCE:** Some agents simply do not know how to accurately price a home. They do not know how to use the data available to provide an accurate assessment to the seller.

2. **APATHY:** The agent fails to do the research and analysis work required to provide accurate advice to the seller and ultimately provides poor counsel.

3. **FEAR OF SELLER:** Many agents lack confidence or preparedness to address the seller's demands of pricing the home too high. The agent would rather have a friendly talk than a business conversation rooted in facts and data.

4. **TO GET NEW BUSINESS:** The best way for any agent to get new business is to get new listings. Listings bring opportunities to meet buyers and others thinking about selling. Some agents will take a listing knowing it is the wrong price just so they can leverage it into new business.

KEY POINTS FROM CHAPTER 4:

1. Overpricing your home by more than 5 percent is the worst mistake you can make.

2. You can have a perfect home, but it will never sell at the wrong price.

3. You can't fool buyers. The consumer has a great deal of data available along with a buyer's agent and an appraiser.

4. Give your listing agent a price he can defend.

5. Don't hire an agent who is willing to overprice your home.

6. Determine base price on specific facts and data rather than emotion.

CHAPTER 5

YOU MAY NOT BE READY TO SELL IF YOU ARE SAYING THESE THINGS

Throughout my years in real estate, I have met many types of sellers and heard many objections when it comes to pricing the home. If you are getting ready to sell your home, see if you fit into any of these "personalities." Then, honestly consider how that might affect your agent's ability to sell your home or the reality of your motivation.

The Defensive Seller: "I am not going to give away my home!"

This comment is usually followed with an unreasonable price tag and a defensive posture with arms crossed.

In a market where approximately 50 percent of homes don't sell, this type of seller likely won't have to worry about giving her house away because she won't get any offers! Being defensive and negatively emotional are counterproductive in the sale of your home. My advice is to hire a great agent and listen to her advice on the value of your home. If her advice is not going to work for you, I would suggest not listing. Certainly, selling your home can be a hassle with home upkeep and showings. Therefore, be open to pricing your home reasonably and getting the home in tip-top shape so all the hassle can be lessened and worthwhile.

The Homeless Seller: "We haven't found anywhere to go yet."

This is a legitimate concern. The problem of waiting to sell until you find the home of your choice is this: you will be "contingent buyers" and your offer could get rejected because of it. Also, the seller may not take you seriously, or you may lose the house to a non-contingent buyer. It is important to list your home and start the process so you will ultimately have a fair estimate of what your sale will net at settlement. My advice would be to list the home, and if it sells too quickly then you have a good problem. You can negotiate with the buyer for a brief "rent back" if you need more time or include a contingency for you, the seller, to find "home of choice."

The Inflexible Seller: "If we don't get our price, then we won't sell."

When trying to sell your home, you have to be open-minded, flexible, and willing to compromise. The inflexible seller is basically wasting his and the agent's time and money by even attempting to sell the home. If the ideal offer doesn't come in, the house will continue to sit on the market. Every seller wants to get the best price for his home, but getting an offer at market value is always better than ending up with no offers and no sale because you were too rigid in overpricing.

The Overextended Seller: "We paid X for the home so we need to get Y."

A buyer doesn't care what a seller paid for the home. The value of a home is based on current market conditions, not what the seller paid in the past. It is not possible to fool the market, so seek other professional advice such as a short-sale attorney if you absolutely have to sell.

The Overly Improved Seller: "All of these renovations add up to X, so that should be my list price."

This is a common misconception among sellers who think that the total cost of renovations can somehow be added to the "base price" of their home. Any renovations you complete on your home should be viewed in two ways: 1) a source of enjoyment or convenience while you live there, and 2) as a potential advantage for getting your home selected over competing listings.

The Squatter Seller: "I don't need to move; I'll just keep the house."

Then why are you selling? Return to your motivation and the driving force behind your motivation to move. Saying "I don't need to move" is a strong statement about your current motivation, but it is typically a frustrated reaction to the projected hassles of selling.

The "As-Is" Seller: "I'm not fixing a thing; the house is "as-is," and I want my price too!"

If you have ever been a buyer, how would you feel about buying a home "as-is" for a premium price? Let's be realistic about the process and walk in a buyer's shoes before going any farther down this path. Getting mechanical defects fixed is basically presumed to be a seller's responsibility unless there is a significant reduction in price. It is typically much cheaper to fix problems than lower the price to make it acceptable for buyers.

The Voyeur Seller: "I want to be here for all the showings to welcome the buyers."

The sales process is well defined, and the sellers' showing their home is not part of the process. It is awkward for all parties when the seller stays at the home and tries to meet the buyers. It is so rare to stay and meet the buyers that this type of activity distracts the potential buyers from seeing themselves in the home.

The Banker Seller: "I will hold a loan for the buyer if they give me X."

Buyers should be prequalified before previewing homes, so this is creative but rarely helpful. Lenders do not permit a silent second loan, so it is not very plausible. This type of offering typically attracts investors or credit-challenged buyers that most sellers would not accept. The buyer usually wants close to 100 percent financing and/or the seller to be in the second-lien position. Bottom line: the seller who suggests this is usually trying to compensate for the fact he has overpriced his home and thinks creative financing will lure in buyers.

KEY POINTS FROM CHAPTER 5:

1. Selling a home requires motivation, flexibility, and compromise.

2. The market determines value, so know the market conditions of your area.

3. Don't put your house on the market if you aren't committed to selling.

SECTION 2

HIRING THE RIGHT AGENT

CHAPTER 6

WHAT IS A LISTING AGENT'S JOB?

Good agents know exactly what to do and have resources to execute a successful listing. They will have a
plan, resources, and well-designed system for selling your
home.

A listing agent has four primary roles:

1. *Preparation before the sale*: Counsel the seller on getting the home ready for sale, provide precise pricing guidance, and set expectations.

2. *Exposure*: Expose the home to the largest possible
   number of buyers.

3. *Negotiation*: Negotiate offers and terms with buyer's agents.

4. *Management*: Manage a smooth transaction to completion.

Let's take each one of these and really understand exactly what should be expected of your agent during the listing and selling process.

Role 1: Preparation before the sale

There are really three important parts to this role:

- Staging the home

- Pricing the home

- Setting expectations about the process

Staging the home

Any real estate professional will need to see your home and do a thorough review of its condition. When you first meet with an agent, be prepared to tell her exactly what you have done to improve the home, any issues about the home's current condition, and things you think make your home unique. After a detailed discussion with you and tour of your home, a top agent will likely offer advice about mechanical issues or blatant cosmetic problems that need to be fixed.

This is not to be confused with the role of a professional stager. A professional stager works with agents and their clients to effectively prepare and showcase houses so that they will appeal to the largest number of potential buyers. Staging is a profession unto itself with a training and development curriculum. A professional agent will offer staging as a service to his or her clients and NOT try to be the stager.

It is very common for an agent to hear these objections from sellers:

1. "I am not going to replace the carpet. They can just make an offer."

2. "Why should I paint when they will come in and pick their own paint colors?"

3. "There is nothing wrong with my house. I have lived here for years and everything works fine."

4. "We have accumulated so much stuff over the years. We don't have anywhere to put all of it."

5. "This neighborhood sells! Buyers know these homes aren't perfect."

I understand the ideas and thoughts behind these commonly expressed objections, but they are not acceptable to the majority of buyers in today's market. If you are working with a genuine professional, he will tell you what you need to do and show you why you need to do it. A true professional will show you other homes in your price range that have made recommended improvements. There is a consequence for not properly preparing your home for sale: unstaged homes typically do not sell as fast as staged homes. Additionally, buyers have a hard time seeing past dated decor and are typically willing to pay more for a move-in-ready home.

In 2012, The Real Estate Staging Association (RESA) studied eighty-nine homes that were not staged before going on the market. These homes sat on the market for an average of 166 days before the homeowners called in a professional home stager. These homes received their first offer, on average, thirty-two days after being professionally staged. This is 81 percent less time on the market. Nine staged homes had multiple offers.

RESA also studied 359 homes in 2012 that were staged before they went on the market. These homes, on average, received their first offer in twenty-six days after being professionally staged. Sixty-nine of the homes received multiple offers.

RESA's conclusion is that you should stage your home before placing it on the market. By doing so, you are likely to sell your home 87 percent faster than if you didn't stage it.

You can also save money by staging your home beforehand. RESA provides a simple formula to determine how much you can save by staging your home. For example, if the monthly expenses for your home are $2,100 and your house sits on the market for six months unstaged, the cost to you is $12,600. However, if the home is staged, the time on the market could be reduced by four months, saving you $8,400. Following are the steps to compute your savings by staging your home:

- Mortgage + expenses (utilities, etc.) = Monthly expenses

- Monthly expenses × six months (average time unstaged) = Cost to list house unstaged

- Monthly expenses × four months (average time on market reduced) – staging fee = Savings if you stage your house first.

Source: The Real Estate Staging Association's report *The Consumer Guide to Real Estate Staging*™ (2012) referenced with their permission.

Figure 6: Before Staging – Living Room

Figure 7: After Staging – Living Room

Figure 8: Before Staging – Bedroom

Figure 9: After Staging – Bedroom

*Before and after staging photos,
courtesy of Catrin Duncan
of Catrin Duncan Interiors.*

In addition to staging your home, I recommend getting a home inspection and fixing any mechanical defects before listing your home. Ask your agent to make sure the completed home inspection and receipts from any repair work are made available to prospective buyers.

I advocate for the prelisting home inspection because:

1. It builds confidence in the buyer's mind about the condition of the home.

2. It builds trust in buyer's mind about the candor of the seller.

3. It is better to do repairs beforehand than having to do them while under contract. The buyer has less reason to walk away, there is less pressure, and it puts the seller in a better place during any negotiations.

Pricing the home

There is nothing more important than pricing your home properly. This is the toughest part of the prelisting process for both the listing agent and the seller. Today's world is so rich with information that fooling a buyer with an unrealistically high price is simply naïve. Playing games with the listing price is a huge mistake. You may have a preconceived notion of your home's value or a "bottom line," but, as we discussed in chapter

4, you don't determine the price. A good agent will work with you to establish the property price and educate you about the role of pricing.

Pricing a home accurately requires multiple sources of data and input. Here are the key factors to review when pricing your home:

1. What is the condition of your home compared to others that have sold?

2. What is the supply-demand for homes similar to your home?

3. What price would cause your home to receive offers within ten showings?

If any of this isn't perfectly clear or agreeable, ask the agent to take you to competing homes in your area. Seeing is believing! Visiting other listed area homes might provide the perfect amount of clarity you need to price your home correctly and expedite getting it sold.

Setting expectations about the process

As a real estate agent, I go through the process of selling and buying homes daily. As homeowners and buyers, you might go through it a few times in your lifetime. It is part of any listing agent's job to help educate and inform you about the home-selling process. The agent should outline what his or her services are from the very beginning and continually communicate with you about the status of your home and the next steps in the process. He or she should help educate you about real estate in today's market, current rules and regulations, and realistic expectations for selling your home in a certain time frame or at a certain price. As the client, you also need to communicate with your agent about any concerns you have and about your expectations. Together, you should come to an agreement on what qualifies as a successful transaction.

Role 2: Exposure

The Internet has thoroughly changed the real estate process! A brief history lesson will quickly show you how the world of marketing properties has changed the sales process forever.

Before the Multiple Listing Service (MLS) was developed, brokers held the listings "in-house," and buyers needed to engage a broker or one of the broker's agents to tap into the "local knowledge" of what was listed. Or buyers could drive around neighborhoods aimlessly looking for signs and open houses.

When the MLS was introduced, it gave agents access to other agents' listings. In an instant, agents could see available listings from all brokerages. Agents could then share these listings with their clients and run reports based on wants and needs. For example, an agent could search for homes with a specific number of bedrooms and baths in any designated town. The MLS was controlled by the brokers, and consumers had zero access to the information. Then the Internet made the MLS data public, and the consumer was given ready access to the information.

The National Association of REALTORS® found that 92 percent of active home buyers receive results from automatic searches for properties that interested them. So the minute your home is listed, 92 percent of buyers can learn about it immediately. Talk about exposure: it doesn't get any better and faster than that!

The Internet has created a need for digital content that is appealing, informative, and presents the home in a favorable light. Nine out of ten home buyers today rely on the Internet as one of their primary research sources, with 52 percent turning to the web as their first step, according to the National Association of REALTORS®' 2012 *Profile of Home Buyers and Sellers*. Your first and most frequent showing is online, so your home needs to look its best and be showcased with many professional photos. There used to be a need to invite people to properties via open houses, raffles, and parties because buyers could not see homes online. In today's world, listings are having a 24-7 open house!

A critical duty of the agent is to make sure the home is presented in a professional and well-photographed manner. The home needs to be presented in a way that justifies the seller's price and motivates the buyer to come visit. If you are not getting showings, you are being rejected online.

Role 3: Negotiation

Most agents claim they are tough negotiators, but how can you really tell? Here are two ways you can measure how strong a negotiator your agent is:

1. Ask the agent to lower his commission. If he says yes, consider another agent! If an agent is unable to negotiate and create value for his own services with his money, how do you think he will negotiate with *your* money? Stop and think about this point. How strong is an agent who gives away his own money and his own value upon a simple request?

2. Ask the agent to show you her sale price to list price ratio, and compare it to the market average. This measures how close to the list price the listing agent was able to get for her clients. It isn't very hard to present a lowball offer and *not* negotiate or create value for the property being sold. The trained professional will have skills and tactics to deliver value to the process.

A good agent should be able to justify his services in the negotiation phase of selling a home. In my local market, I am 8 percent better than the market average of what other agents get when they sell a home versus when I sell a home. My average home sales price is almost $800,000 which means I average $64,000 in better returns for my sellers than the average agent. In chapter 1, I made a concrete point that the industry norm for commission is 3 percent *regardless* of track record or talent. If you are going to pay the same wage, then it is wise to select the very best agent available to you in your area to represent your investment.

Agents are not all created equally. You should select the one with the best credentials and statistics to back up her claims of being a skilled negotiator!

Role 4: Manage a smooth transaction to closing

Buying and selling a home is usually an emotional process. For sure, emotions run high when you combine money and family needs. A good agent is able to manage any emotions that can become toxic to a deal and potentially lead to its failing. This is where the agent's personality comes into play again. It is extremely important that you have a trusting and comfortable relationship with your agent. You need someone who will always be honest with you and very supportive throughout the entire process.

Additionally, real estate agents and their assistants handle a lot of details with every transaction. There are a lot of steps and processes that go into selling or buying a home. After all, it is a huge financial purchase! To manage the details for all my transactions, I use a comprehensive transaction management system with checklists, follow-ups, and task management, plus a timeline highlighting the key dates in the contract (Figure 10). My clients genuinely appreciate the timeline because it gives them a visual and an understanding of what needs to happen by when.

Make sure your agent has a reliable and well-developed system to manage the sale or purchase of your home from beginning to end.

CONTRACTUAL TIMELINE

DATE	DAYS	ACTION ITEM	DAYS UNTIL CLOSING
5/23/2013		Contract Acceptance	38
5/24/2013	1		37
5/25/2013	2		36
5/26/2013	3		35
5/27/2013	4		34
5/28/2013	5		33
5/29/2013	6		32
5/30/2013	7		31
5/31/2013	8		30
6/1/2013	9		29
6/2/2013	10	Loan Application Completed	28
6/3/2013	11		27
6/4/2013	12		26
6/5/2013	13		25
6/6/2013	14	Inspections Completed	24
6/7/2013	15		23
6/8/2013	16		22
6/9/2013	17		21
6/10/2013	18		20
6/11/2013	19		19
6/12/2013	20	HOA Documents Due	18
6/13/2013	21		17
6/14/2013	22		16
6/15/2013	23		15
6/16/2013	24		14
6/17/2013	25		13
6/18/2013	26		12
6/19/2013	27		11
6/20/2013	28		10
6/21/2013	29		9
6/22/2013	30	Appraisal Complete & Loan Commitment	8
6/23/2013	31		7
6/24/2013	32		6
6/25/2013	33		5
6/26/2013	34		4
6/27/2013	35		3
6/28/2013	36		2
6/29/2013	37		1
6/30/2013	38	Settlement	0

Figure 10: Sample timeline highlighting the key dates in the contract.

KEY POINTS FROM CHAPTER 6:

1. Prepare your home and don't cut corners. Do it right if you want to get the most money in the shortest amount of time.

2. Don't overprice your home.

3. Demand terrific photography.

4. Select an agent with a track record of being a tough negotiator.

5. Make sure your agent is committed to a successful transaction from start to finish.

CHAPTER 7

TWENTY-ONE QUESTIONS EVERY SELLER SHOULD ASK HIS OR HER AGENT

1. **How long have you been a real estate agent?**
    I advise that you hire an experienced agent. When selecting an agent, I would highly recommend finding an agent with at least five years of experience and at least seventy-five to one hundred listings sold. If you meet a terrific agent who is new to the business, ask him to partner with a more experienced agent from his office.

2. **Are you a full-time agent?**
    This is a great question to gauge how serious an agent is about his or her business. If an agent is part time, then how will he be able to service client inquiries, stay current on laws, and respond to

your needs? This question may seem silly, but it is so easy to get licensed that many people have a license. However, they only work real estate on a very limited basis. Think about it: They are applying for the job of handling your largest asset, but will only be available part time.

3. **What are your business hours?**
Buyers want information quickly. It is important for agents to have support that can assist buyers with information about your property. Being available and ready to serve is an important service provided by the brokerage offices and/or the agent's direct team.

4. **How do you rank within your firm?**
It is important to work with a top agent. Ask for the actual sales results for the last twelve months from the office where the agent works. Agents charge the same rates to sell a home, so work with a proven, successful agent.

5. **Do you work alone or with a team?**
Teams are a great way to improve customer service and leverage talents of different individuals. Most agents need support in the key areas of their business: buyers, listings, and closings. A successful agent will have at least an executive assistant to assist with the tremendous amount of administrative work required to successfully sell a home and likely other staff to enhance the client experience. A busy

agent working alone may not have enough time to devote to your questions or details of the sale.

6. **What do you see as your role in selling my home?**
Being able to communicate a plan is an essential part of being a successful listing agent. An agent who is unable to tell you specifically what will be done during the listing phase is probably not equipped. In chapter 6, I mentioned the four roles of an agent: counsel before the sale, expose the home to the most buyers possible, negotiate offers, and manage a smooth closing.

7. **How many transactions have you completed in the last twelve months?**
This is like asking your surgeon, "How many surgeries have you done?" It is important to work with a professional who is experienced and closes lots of transactions. When things get turbulent, you will want an agent who can handle the emotions, challenges, and objections from all parties. Having an experienced listing agent who sells a lot of homes is typically your best selection since they have "been there, done that," and weathered many tough transactions.

8. **What is your list price to sales price ratio?**
This is a critically important statistic. It lets you know immediately if this agent has a track record of being honest about the list price and how well she negotiates. For example, an agent who sells a

lot of homes but has a sales price to list price ratio of 78 percent means she gets only 78 percent (on average) of the original list price. This type of agent tells sellers their home is worth a lot more than it really is. Sellers want to believe it, but they are disappointed at the closing table. Caution: don't always listen to the agent who tells you the highest price.

9. **What percentage of your listings do you sell?**
A successful agent should sell at least 80 to 90 percent of his or her listings. There are going to be valid situations where sellers choose not to move or take their home off the market. If an agent has failed to sell homes in the past twelve months, it is imperative to ask why.

10. **How many days do your listings stay on the market before selling?**
The shocking reality is that homes sell much faster than you would suspect, even in down markets. A close look at the data will reveal that homes generally sell within 100 days. If an agent takes longer than 100 to 120 days to sell homes, there is likely a problem. Ask the agent to provide the market average and his or her average time to sell homes.

11. **What is your system for following up on sign calls or Internet leads?**
Buyer leads need to be called immediately. The National Association of REALTORS®' 2012 *Profile of Home Buyers and Sellers* tells us that buyers are

searching online for three weeks before engaging an agent. These buyers want to find a deal themselves so when they call or e-mail after seeing a yard sign or online listing, agents need to act quickly. A successful agent will have a specific system for his or her team to respond immediately to new leads and a system to follow up on those leads.

12. How many websites will you advertise my home on?

There are great services these days that syndicate listings so they appear on hundreds of real estate websites. The service I use is called List Hub. Make sure your agent is subscribing to a syndication service to provide maximum exposure for your listing. The buyers are online, and this is a part of selling that must be taken very seriously. The technology is simple; the cost is typically prohibitive for rookie agents. Don't risk it. By all means, make sure your agent is subscribed to a syndication service.

13. Do you use a professional photographer or take photos yourself?

Have you ever looked online at houses? What are you looking at? Obviously, you are looking at photographs, and you probably have realized that the homes with excellent photographs draw you in and make you curious. Contrast that to the home with blurry photographs that make you think the seller is hiding something. Having excellent photography is an absolute must! An agent is not a photographer and shouldn't pretend to be one. Professional photography can make or break whether you "make the list" of homes buyers would like to preview.

14. How do I cancel my listing agreement if I am not satisfied?
It is absolutely fair to have a "cancellation clause" for your listing agreement. If you want to sever a relationship, you should be able to do it with just cause, and you should be ready to pay the agent for her services. Listing agreements are bilateral, and both parties need to do their part. Locking a homeowner into a one-year agreement is just preposterous, inappropriate, and unfair. Take a look at the data: if your home hasn't sold in the first 120 days, then you probably won't be selling your home without some major adjustments.

15. How much do you spend on marketing each month?
As a successful agent, I spend over $100,000 annually on marketing. Successful businesses spend money on advertising and marketing. Plain and simple! An agent without a marketing budget is not running a successful business. This question will expose the agent's commitment to marketing and advertising his listings.

16. How many listings do you currently have listed?
Having a lot of listings is a good thing! Listings bring buyers of all kinds, and an agent's job is to know who is in the market and match them to properties. I typically carry dozens of listings so I know from the showing activity in a specific area or price point, exactly which agents are working with buyers, and the level of demand. This is a huge advantage for my sellers. Work with an agent who has a lot of listings, knows what is going on, and has a team that supports his or her business.

17. Why should I list my home with you?
Listen to the first thing the agent says. You will likely hear what he thinks he does best. This is a really telling question about the professional you are about to hire, so sit quietly and listen to his response. The correct answer should be supported by facts and data. If the agent's answer is something ambiguous like, "You can always get a hold of me," then consider whether he has the depth to be your representative. Listen for a response with substance and depth supported by facts and data.

18. Will you provide a list of ten recent sellers for me to contact?
Any successful agent can easily and quickly provide references. This should not be a struggle at all. Make sure to call some of these references and ask how the agent handled her roles as a listing agent. Did the agent help prepare the sellers to sell the

home with good advice about staging and pricing? Did she attract buyers and expose the home professionally to the market? Did she negotiate well on the seller's behalf? Did she manage the transaction through the inspections and closing successfully?

19. What percentage of your business comes from referrals?

Past performance is usually a good indicator of future success. If an agent is working by referral, he is typically reliable and shows care for his clients.

20. How will you keep me informed about showings, feedback, and new homes on the market that affect my sale?

When your home is listed, it is very exciting, but having showings is also nerve-racking. Naturally, you will want to hear about how things went. Successful agents will have a system for obtaining feedback after a showing. Feedback is not instantaneous, so it is important for agents to have a detailed follow-up plan. Good agents will also be constantly watching the market and communicating with you about your home's competition.

21. Will you ask me to lower the price of my home if we aren't getting offers?

A truthful and honest agent will answer without hesitation, "Yes!" A competent professional has the integrity to confront challenging topics and also has the insight to make adjustments. If your home isn't selling, obviously the buyers don't think it is worth the asking price. In fact, they don't even think the pricing is realistic enough to make an offer. Pricing is a very sensitive topic, and a strong, professional agent should be hired to sell your home and tell you exactly what needs to be done to sell in your market area.

KEY POINTS FROM CHAPTER 7:

1. Ask a lot of questions.

2. Look for substantive answers.

3. You owe it to yourself to hire the best.

4. This is a huge financial and emotional decision; hire an experienced professional!

SECTION 3

GETTING READY TO SELL

CHAPTER 8

THE "HONEY-DO" LIST

It is definitely true: "You only have one chance to make a first impression." You would wash and vacuum your car before you sold it. The same is true with selling your home. This chapter contains specific things sellers should do if they want to maximize potential for selling and return on investment.

I frequently get the phone call, "We aren't ready to sell yet, but we want you to come over and tell us what we need to do to get ready to sell." What I really hear them saying is, "I know I have a lot of clutter and deferred maintenance, so please come over and give me a to-do list." This is awesome; the market rewards conscientious sellers.

Since the majority of sellers know they need to get the home in showing condition, I have come up with a four-step process: fix it, straighten it, clean it, and finish it.

EXTERIOR AND YARD

Fix it

- ❏ Replace porch lighting, if damaged, worn, or broken
- ❏ Repaint the front door
- ❏ Replace worn door handles
- ❏ Make sure sprinklers and water hoses work
- ❏ Restain or repaint the deck, if worn
- ❏ Repair damaged fencing and gates
- ❏ Repair any damaged shutters, gutters, siding, and roof shingles
- ❏ Repair, secure, and/or replace any stair railings
- ❏ Repaint or replace the mailbox, if needed

Straighten it

- ❏ Mow, weed, and water regularly to keep your lawn looking its best
- ❏ Store any yard supplies or tools in the garage or a shed
- ❏ Remove any toys, shoes, or miscellaneous items from the yard, front porch, patio, or deck
- ❏ Remove any dead plants
- ❏ Trim bushes and trees

❏ Place trash cans at the back of house or off to the side, out of the initial line of sight

Clean it

❏ Power wash the exterior of the house
❏ Wash windows inside and out
❏ Keep walkways swept and clear
❏ Clean outdoor furniture and cushions, or replace if damaged and worn
❏ Clean the pool or hot tub, if applicable and in season

Finish it

❏ Add fresh mulch and seasonal, colorful plants
❏ Add a new and welcoming front doormat
❏ Add or freshen up outdoor seating areas
❏ Make house numbers easily visible

KITCHENS AND BATHROOMS

Fix it

❏ Update appliances, if possible, or make sure they are in proper working condition
❏ Replace any damaged or missing floor tiles
❏ Tighten or replace loose or broken cabinet hardware
❏ Repair any leaks, damaged cabinets, sinks, doors, etc.

❏ Recaulk around showers, tubs, sinks, etc., if damaged or discolored

❏ Touch up the paint, if painted recently, or repaint with a neutral color to freshen up the space

Straighten it

❏ Remove as many items as possible from bathroom vanities and around bathtubs

❏ Organize items neatly in drawers, cabinets, closets, and on shelving

❏ Remove appliances you do not use daily from the kitchen counter tops. Kitchen counter tops should be as clear as possible so they look spacious

❏ Remove magnets and papers from the exterior of the refrigerator

Clean it

❏ Clean every surface very, very well, including lighting fixtures; bathrooms and kitchens should be extremely clean for every showing

❏ Clean tile grout and remove any stains from surfaces

❏ Remove any scuff marks from the walls

Finish it

❏ Put down a new rug—one by the kitchen sink and one by the shower/tub is all that is usually needed

❏ Add a scented candle to the bathroom vanity and fresh towels
❏ Put up a new shower liner, and a curtain if damaged
❏ Add a plant above the refrigerator or place on the counter top

BEDROOMS

Fix it

❏ Replace stained or worn carpets, if possible, or deep clean
❏ Repair any wall damage
❏ Repair any closet or lighting fixtures
❏ Touch up the paint, if painted recently, or repaint with a neutral color to freshen up the space

Straighten it

❏ Hang clothes neatly in the closet or folded in dresser drawers, but resist packing too many into the space
❏ Store out-of-season clothes, or donate unused clothing
❏ Store excess furniture elsewhere
❏ Remove personal items from dresser tops and nightstands
❏ Remove personal photos
❏ Organize and neatly store children's toys

Clean it

- ❏ Wash or dry-clean curtains and bed linens
- ❏ Dust furniture and clean the floor
- ❏ Clean lighting fixtures

Finish it

- ❏ Add decorative pillows to the beds
- ❏ Make the beds for photos and showings
- ❏ Open curtains to let the light in for photos and showings

LIVING AND DINING AREAS

Fix it

- ❏ Repair any wall damage, including nail holes from pictures
- ❏ Touch up the paint, if painted recently, or repaint with a neutral color to freshen up the space
- ❏ Make sure all systems are in good working order, such as heating and air conditioning, fireplace, security, well, septic, doorbells, electrical outlets, garage door, etc.

Straighten it

- ❏ Remove any personal photos, trophies, or mementos

❏ Straighten items on bookshelves and in cabinets and closets

❏ Remove excess paper catalogs, magazines, books, etc.

❏ Store extra furniture pieces and other household items in a storage facility to make rooms look larger and allow for easy flow

❏ Use a minimalist approach when it comes to decorating the fireplace mantle and coffee table and setting the dining table

❏ Rearrange furniture so that it creates conversational areas; the main seating area should be facing toward the focal point of the room, such as the fireplace or beautiful view

Clean it

❏ Polish and clean furniture, floors, curtains, and linens

❏ Clean lighting fixtures and dust off cabinets and pictures

Finish it

❏ Turn on all the lights for photos and showings, and add additional lamps, if needed

❏ Open all the curtains to let the natural light in for photos and showings

❏ Add fresh flowers to the dining room table and a table runner

❏ Add a few decorative pillows to the seating areas

It is a lot of work, but the effort increases the probability of getting an offer in the shortest amount of time for the most amount of money. Would a true professional let you list a home without telling you to fix it, straighten it, clean it, and finish it? A professional real estate agent would not allow a seller to just list a home without explaining why a home needs to show really well to get maximum exposure, maximum potential to be selected, and maximum return on investment. Those three things are why you are hiring an agent, so make sure you get a specific action plan for your home.

KEY POINTS FROM CHAPTER 8:

1. Fix it, straighten it, clean it, finish it.

2. Depersonalize your home; make it look and feel more like an inviting hotel suite.

3. You probably won't get any offers if you don't take the time to make your home look warm and inviting.

4. You will have to fix things after the inspection anyway, so do them ahead for maximum benefit.

5. You are more likely to get a higher offer sooner if you get your home ready to sell when listed.

You will be disproportionately punished for not being prepared

6. Ask your agent for a list of trustworthy contractors or handymen.

CHAPTER 9

SHOW TIME!!!

You have rented a storage unit for extra household items, cleaned your home thoroughly, fixed any outstanding repairs or overdue maintenance, and staged your home to sell. Your listing agent and you have decided it is time to officially list the home. What happens now? Hopefully, you will receive requests to open your home for showings, where buyer's agents walk through the home with prospective buyers.

Agents typically use a showing service, such as Centralized Showing Service (CSS) to coordinate showing requests with buyer's agents and sellers. By using a showing service, buyer's agents calling to request showings can avoid having to track down listing agents. The staff at the showing service have greater availability and can contact all necessary parties, as needed, to get a showing scheduled. As a seller, this means it is easier for buyers to come view your home, leading to a greater chance for a sale.

Through the service I use, CSS, there are three types of showings:

- **Go:** This means that buyers can go view the home whenever they wish, without coordinating with the listing agent or sellers. The "Go" type showing is generally used for vacant homes.

- **Courtesy:** This means that a representative from CSS will contact the listing agent and seller, using the contact information provided, to inform them about the showing request. The seller will be told when the showing will occur, not asked if the time is convenient for them. The buyer's agent already has approval to show the home.

- **Appointment Required:** This means that a representative from CSS will contact the seller or the listing agent to obtain approval for the buyer's agent to show the home at a certain time. CSS must get the listing agent's or the seller's approval before the buyer's agent can show the home to his prospective buyer.

According to CSS, the "Go" and "Courtesy" showing types get more showings, on average, per week than the

"Appointment Required" type. Showing notifications can be communicated via phone or e-mail, and agents and sellers can approve requests via phone, e-mail, or text messages. You decide up front if you want to approve all showing requests or if the agent can provide approval. Your listing agent should discuss with you what showing type would work best for your home and what would make you the most comfortable. However, it is extremely important to be flexible. If you want your home sold, you have to make it available, even if it is a hassle to do so.

The previous chapter provided checklists for preparing your home for sale by making it look its absolute best. Below is a showing checklist that you can use to properly prepare for each showing.

Showing Checklist

- ❑ Open all the curtains for daytime showings; close curtains for nighttime showings

- ❑ Turn on all the lights

- ❑ Play soft instrumental music

- ❑ Make all the beds

❏ Tidy up all areas

❏ Put away any personal documents or items, such as bank and credit card statements

❏ Wipe down the sink, kitchen counters, and bathroom vanities

❏ Flush all toilets and put down toilet seats

❏ Empty the garbage, litter boxes, and any items that may produce odors

❏ Remove tools, toys, pet feces, etc. from the yard

❏ Clear walkways and driveways

❏ Leave your house before the showing and, if possible, take pets with you or safely secure them

Keeping up with all the cleaning and straightening while your home is on the market can be exhausting. Think about it. Your home has to look pristine for all showings. You could get a call for a showing to occur at any time, and you may have only an hour to get out the door before the buyers arrive. That isn't much time, which means you can't have a long list of things to do within that time frame.

Tips to Lessen the Stress of Showings

Here are some tips to help lessen the stress when you get a showing request:

Be excited that you received a request for a showing. Someone is interested in seeing your home!

However, don't get your hopes up and expect an instant offer. Nevertheless, showings are a good thing because they give you the opportunity to get feedback about your home and can provide valuable data that can be used to adjust your home's position in the market, if needed. As discussed in chapter 4, pricing can have a direct effect on whether or not your home gets any showings in the first place. If your home's price position is off, buyers will either not request showings or not advance in the process and make an offer on your home. A showing request can indicate buyers' interest, and the lack of an offer can indicate that the price is potentially off the mark.

Remove as much from the home as possible.

When you were going through your "honey-do" list to prepare your house for listing, you may have hesitated putting many of your items in storage. But remember that each item you decide to keep in your house is an item you will need to either keep clean or move out of the way to clean. If you truly don't need the item, whether it is a chair, a book, a stack of papers, or a favorite knickknack, store it while your house is the market. The less cluttered your house looks, the less time it is likely to be on the market!

Use fewer rooms in your home.

We tend to spread ourselves out in our homes. In other words, we tend to fill up and use all the rooms in our homes, even if the house is much bigger than our previous residence. The more rooms we use, the more we have to clean. While your home is on the market, if possible, see if there are rooms you don't really need to use either at all or daily. For example, if your house has three bathrooms, do you need to use all three or could you get by for a short time using two, leaving the third one clean and ready for showings at all times? If there is any way to make an adjustment in your lifestyle for a short time to reduce the amount of upkeep in your home, try it out. Remember, being open-minded and flexible will only help your home sell quicker and make the process less stressful.

Clean and tidy up frequently.

When you are finished using something, put it away. When you are finished eating a meal, wipe down the table, clean the dishes, and put everything away. When you bring in the mail, sort through it and recycle or file it right away.

When your children are done playing with their toys, make sure the toys are put away. When your main entrance or foyer gets dirty, perhaps after a rainy day, clean it as soon as possible. Try to not wear shoes in the house to reduce dirt being tracked through the home. The list can go on and on, but the point is to try to constantly be proactive and disciplined. It is not easy, but it will make leaving the house for a showing much easier.

———————

Feedback

Following a showing you will probably be wondering how it went. Did they like the house? Will they make an offer? The waiting can be difficult, but the feedback is not immediate. Your listing agent should have a system for obtaining feedback from showings and communicating that feedback to you. Some buyer's agents provide feedback via a showing survey after the showing, but many have to be continually contacted and reminded. It is your listing agent's job to try to obtain as much feedback as possible.

The following are the types of feedback you want to obtain about your home:

- Buyer's overall impression of the home and its location

- Buyer's overall interest compared to other properties they have seen

- Buyer's and buyer's agent opinions on the price of the property

- Buyer's potential next step (e.g., request a second showing, make an offer, considering the property, or not considering the property)

- Any other comments that might help sell the home, such as features the buyers liked and issues identified when viewing the home (e.g., unpleasant smells or damage)

Hearing feedback about your home can be either rewarding or difficult. Positive comments such as "The home is immaculate" or "The craftsmanship is outstanding" or "The kitchen is a chef's dream" will surely make you feel good about your home and the hard work you have put into it. It is the negative comments that can be hard to hear. Try not to take it personally; everyone has different tastes, wants, and needs. However, since you need your home to be desirable to the greatest number of potential buyers possible, you need to be open to listening for ways to improve it. Your agent should help you interpret the feedback and provide a plan of action for using the feedback to improve the home's marketability. For my clients, I provide a weekly report that includes their home's position in the market (pricing and competition), history and feedback of showings, and online traffic statistics (Figure 11).

Figure 11: Sample weekly feedback report.

Here are some questions to consider when reviewing feedback, but the questions will vary based on your home's feedback:

- Does the price need to be adjusted?

- Does your home need a deep cleaning?

- Do you need to remove more items from your home to make it appear more spacious?

- Do you need to increase the curb appeal with some yard work and gardening?

- Are there simple and inexpensive changes you could make that could improve the look or functionality of the home? It could be as a simple as a fresh coat of paint!

The market determines the value of your home. Even if you think it looks perfect and is priced right, it is the market that will have the final say. Listen to the feedback and your agent's advice to help you make the right decisions that will ultimately get your home sold.

KEY POINTS FROM CHAPTER 9:

1. Work with an agent who has a system or service for coordinating showing requests.

2. Discuss with your agent the appropriate showing type for your home.

3. Use a checklist and develop a routine to manage the moments before a showing.

4. Discuss feedback with your listing agent on a weekly basis to make timely decisions about your home and its position in the market.

SECTION 4

SEALING THE DEAL

CHAPTER 10

"HONEY, WE GOT AN OFFER!!"

"Congratulations, your home has been selected by a buyer as a home they would like to buy and live in." Let me repeat that sentence. **"Congratulations, your home has been selected by a buyer as a home they would like to buy and live in."** Think about the importance of this sentence. A buyer is willing to spend her hard-earned money on your home. That is flattering REGARDLESS of the offer price. The price is a function of the market; the buyer's offer represents her desire to buy YOUR home. Too often I see sellers react negatively to an offer. This is shocking to me. They have probably had showings and been completely inconvenienced by buyers who have come through their home, wasted their time, and not made an offer, but they get upset with the people who do make an offer. Anger serves no purpose in a negotiation, so my professional advice is to embrace a written offer and try your hardest to make it work.

The first person to write an offer is almost always the person who likes your home the most. She has taken the time to write an offer and likely really wants your home. "Your first offer is your best offer" is typically true unless the buyer is an investor or the home is requiring major renovations. As you begin to review an offer, it is always my advice to review the offer with a fine-tooth comb.

A professional agent will take the time to review a contract and will also come prepared with:

- a summation sheet of the offer

- a breakdown of the fees with a clear bottom-line figure of your proceeds

- recommendations based on facts of the marketplace

- a list of what to expect next

- an update on similar sales to help gauge validity of the offer

These pieces are important as you begin to review the written agreement.

THE CONTRACT

You are frequently asked to read agreements and sign documents for various reasons, including medical documentation, insurance, vehicle and home purchases, new accounts, etc. Do you really take the time to *read* what you are signing? Do you even understand what you are reading and signing? When you want to sell your home or buy a new home, the amount of paperwork to review and sign can be daunting. Just one look at the stack of papers that make up the real estate contract can be overwhelming, and then you have to interpret it! Your patience may wear thin, but this is not the time to blindly sign paperwork. The many forms you need to sign are there for your benefit and protection. A good real estate professional will review and thoroughly explain the various documents and forms with you before you sign. Understand what you are signing and agreeing to before picking up a pen. If you don't understand something, speak up and ask your agent to explain the terms again.

As the seller, you may see the sales price you want on the contract and be ready to sign, but buried in the contract are contingencies that may have you thinking twice about the deal. Your agent should review with you all the terms of the contract, including the offer price, any request for closing cost assistance, financing, home inspections, appraisals, required homeowner's association documentation, the requested settlement date, the various ways the buyer can get out of the contract, and any other terms.

Your agent should outline the key dates for you so that you know what needs to happen when. In chapter 6, I provided a sample of the timeline I provide to my clients so they can easily follow the real estate transaction process. The timeline highlights the key dates in the contract. **Those key dates are critical and are tied to the contingencies within the contract. Missing any of those dates can make the contract null and void.**

To help reduce some of the mystery around the real estate contract, here is an explanation of the main key dates within a typical contract. Contracts may have additional contingencies and dates, depending on the nature of the deal. Always consult with your agent and review the documentation carefully. Selling your home can be an exciting time for you; don't let your emotions cloud your judgment and attention to detail!

Contract Acceptance Date This is the date when the contract was accepted by the second party in the transaction. In the simplest scenario, the buyer will submit a contract, and the day the seller accepts it is the contract acceptance date. Along with the contract, the buyer will provide a deposit to be held in escrow, typically by the buyer's broker, until settlement.

If the seller is interested in the buyer's offer but wants to modify some of the contract terms such as sales price, settlement date, contingency periods, etc., the seller can submit a counteroffer. The buyer can then accept the counteroffer, ratifying the contract. This date becomes the contract acceptance date.

However, the buyer may also continue to negotiate by countering. Once both parties have agreed on all terms, you have a ratified contract. Either party may also decide to reject the offer, resulting in no contract acceptance.

Loan Application Completion Date This is the date that the buyer must have a formal, written loan application submitted to a lender. This must be completed within a certain number of days from contract acceptance, typically about five to seven days.

Inspections Completion Date This date states when all the inspections, excluding termite, must be completed. In the contract, the buyer states which type of inspections he wants to do and how many days he has to complete them. Typically, the inspections must be completed within ten to fourteen days of the contract acceptance date. Once the inspections are completed, the buyer's agent will review the inspection reports with the buyers and submit a home inspection repair addendum to the listing agent to discuss with the sellers. The sellers will then have a certain number of days to respond to the repair requests. If the sellers agree to fix everything, the transaction moves forward. If the sellers do not, the buyers will be given a certain number of days to further negotiate, accept the seller's response, or terminate the contract. The home inspection addendum may also state that the buyer can terminate the contract for "no stated reason," such as general dissatisfaction with the home inspection results. Make sure you understand and review all these details with your agent before agreeing and signing.

A termite inspection by a licensed exterminator is also completed before settlement to determine if there is termite or other wood-destroying insect infestation or damage. If damage or active infestation is found, the seller is required to pay for the repairs and/or treatment up to 2 percent of the sales price. If the repair cost exceeds 2 percent, the seller may cancel the contract unless the buyer agrees to pay for the additional repair costs.

Homeowner's Association Documents Due If the home for sale is part of a homeowner's association (HOA) or condominium association, the seller is required to obtain a copy of all the related association's documentation and provide it to the listing agent. The buyer's agent will send all the documentation to the buyers, who must review it and sign the HOA addendum within a certain number of days. If the buyer does not agree to the rules and regulations set forth in the homeowner's or condominium association documentation, he or she can terminate the contract. As a seller, you should obtain your association's documentation and make sure your agent submits it and obtains the required signatures as soon as possible.

Appraisal Ordered Date The buyer, or his or her lender, must order an appraisal within a certain number of days from contract acceptance, if there is an appraisal addendum in the contract that defines this. The appraisal needs to be completed for loan commitment to occur, if the transaction is contingent on the buyer obtaining a loan.

Loan Commitment Date This date indicates when the buyer needs to have obtained written loan commitment from his or her lender. This must be obtained within a certain number of days from contract acceptance. This date is typically close to the settlement date as this process can take thirty to forty-five days. Make sure your agent is constantly checking with the buyer's agent and/or lender to make sure the process is progressing smoothly and in a timely manner.

If the buyer cannot receive loan commitment within the allotted time frame, the contract is voidable by either party. If the buyer declares the contract null and void, he or she must provide written evidence from the lender that financing was denied. The buyer is entitled to a full refund of his or her deposit, if the buyer has fully complied with the terms of the contract. The buyer may also change the financing terms as long as it does not jeopardize loan approval, change the settlement date, or increase costs to the seller.

Settlement Date This is the day when the transaction will be closed. The sellers, buyers, listing agent, buyer's agent, and title company attorney are typically present for the closing or settlement. The settlement date, time, and location are chosen by the buyer. Any change to this date must be agreed to in writing.

THE BALANCE BETWEEN PRICE AND TERMS

Once you have read the contract completely and have asked questions, it will likely be discovered that the offer has two parts: price and terms. Below is a diagram of the typical relationship between price and terms:

Figure 12: The best price may not come with the best terms and vice versa.

On one side of the scale we have the price and on the other side we have the terms. If you desire the very best price then you will likely have to be flexible with the terms. In contrast, if you want extraordinary terms then you will likely need to be flexible with your price. Let me explain further:

1. GREAT TERMS Imagine you absolutely needed to close on your home within thirty days. A buyer's offer to purchase with a contingency to sell his home would not work with your timeline. You will need superior terms, and in exchange, the buyer will certainly not expect to pay full price.

2. GREAT PRICE Imagine you get a full price offer, but the buyer wants to sell her home first, wants to close in 180 days, and asks you to replace the roof. The price is great, but the terms are not as desirable.

Everyone dreams of a 1) full price offer, 2) no repairs, 3) and a quick closing. The trifecta offer is very rare and is not a reasonable expectation. Offers vary greatly and all things need to be considered. Determine what you truly value in the sale of the home and try to get the very best for yourself in that particular part of the offer.

HANDLING THE OFFER

When an offer is received, the listing agent should reply quickly to the buyer's agent with four key pieces of information:

1. Thank her for the offer.

2. Inform her when the offer will be presented.

3. Inform her when a signed counter will be delivered.

4. Request background about the buyers.

It is my strong suggestion to move rapidly through a counteroffer to keep the buyer interested and excited. Most buyers find it to be an annoyance and gamesmanship when an offer isn't replied to within twenty-four hours. As an agent who also works with buyers, I can tell the readers of this book that without question it is the wrong strategy to move slowly. Remember, these buyers like your home, so you don't want them to sour on the home because dealing with you is difficult.

Sellers often think that since they received one offer another will be right around the corner. Multiple offers situations are so infrequent it is not necessary to discuss them. One offer is just that: it is the only offer, so work your hardest to make a deal with these buyers. The listing agent should have background about the buyers and be able to convey why they have selected your home to purchase. Knowing a buyer's search history, length of time searching, financial capabilities, and why they love your home is critical to maximizing a negotiation. A professional listing agent will have all the details, should present the offer without emotion, and put all the facts in order logically and concisely.

When you are ready to make your counteroffer, I always suggest signing it so the buyer is only a couple of initials away from closing the deal. In addition, I think it is most professional to share comparable home sales being used to defend the counteroffer. It is not professional to think that randomly countering with price bumps is logical or credible. Remove emotion and stick to the facts driving the offer. What is fair market value and why? What are prevailing and normal terms for offers in the marketplace? If a buyer and seller are well educated by their respective agents, then an agreeable deal should come together rather quickly.

CAUTION! A counteroffer means you are rejecting the original offer and attempting to create a new agreement. If the buyer does not wish to accept your counteroffer, then they have every right to walk away from buying the home.

We all want to negotiate, but sometimes it is best to sign a good offer and move forward. I pride myself on being a tough negotiator, but it is prudent to also be a smart negotiator. Again, be true to your intentions of selling. If you reach a stalemate in a negotiation, then try to find common ground before accentuating the points of difference. Negotiations are built on agreement, and it is very common to find agreement on almost all the points. Don't lose a deal over one or two minor details. Cooler heads or creative minds can easily bridge small differences. Isolate the issues and build agreement.

It is often overlooked when negotiating offers that a home inspection will occur and those items will also need to be negotiated. Very few homes are perfect and very few buyers buy "as-is." If you are the seller, then you will need to be ready for inspection items to be addressed, or address your resistance in the contract negotiation. If you are giving up on price, then it is totally acceptable to mark the contract "as-is." This is a perfect example of the price and terms relationship.

SIX TIPS FOR A SMOOTH CLOSING

Once an agreement has been reached, I recommend the following six tips for a smooth closing:

Know Everyone's Role

This sounds easier than it is. There are multiple parties that need to perform in a real estate closing: the lender, the appraiser, the HOA, the buyer's agent, the buyers, the listing agent, the sellers, the movers, the home inspector, the termite inspector, the septic inspector, the surveyor, the title attorney, the homeowners-insurance carrier, and other professionals as needed. I have listed at least fourteen professionals who will be involved in a closing. There are many moving parts to professionally managing a closing, which is why I have emphasized in previous chapters that an agent with staff is more equipped to handle all the details and provide superior service. It is unlikely that one person can do it all; details will be missed.

Follow the Timeline

The dates in a contract are the most critical elements of the agreement and these dates should drive all activities during the contract phase. I have provided a sample timeline we provide our clients during a transaction. This is a very helpful tool for them to reference and make sure we are on track. My staff and I check the dates daily to make sure we are protecting our client's best interest. You should be able to prepare to leave your current home and move to your new home without the worry of the deal falling through because of a missed deadline.

Be Responsive

There will be many details that need to be attended to, and the best way to ensure a smooth transaction is by being responsive and communicative. In my office we like to say, "Communication is the lubrication." A real estate transaction from contract signing to actual closing is usually only thirty to forty-five days long, so it imperative to work closely with your agent. An experienced agent is able to guide his or her client as they navigate the course of the closing process.

Review Title Immediately

Title work needs to be reviewed and cleared as quickly as possible. A title defect or boundary dispute can threaten a transaction and require considerable time to get resolved. In a transaction that takes only thirty to forty-five days from start to finish, managing through a legal maze can sometimes take longer. Your agent should contact the title company as soon as possible once the contract is ratified. The title attorney should "pull" title immediately and review it for any defects, judgments, and liens. A professional agent with significant experience will know how to resolve issues resulting from title discrepancies and have attorneys in his contact database ready to assist.

Get the Repairs Done

If the home inspection finds a couple items needing repair (which is totally normal), then get those done quickly. Do not wait until the last minute and rush around trying to find a contractor. It is important to get the items done and provide the repair receipts to the buyer's agent very soon after agreeing to the work being completed. A bad walk-through is completely unacceptable in our business. It shows a great deal of disrespect for the buyers and for all the service professionals who have done their absolute best to ensure a timely closing. Trying to cut corners or being cheap is in very poor taste. Likely, the agreed-upon items are fair and reasonable, so my recommendation is to always have the items repaired professionally by licensed contractors.

Stay Organized

It never ceases to amaze me how many agents show up with completely unorganized folders or ask for copies of signed documents in the middle of a transaction. It is grossly unprofessional, and I am not sure how an unorganized agent can lead his client through a settlement successfully if he is ill prepared. A professional agent will have provided her client with very specific timelines and constantly touch base to let the client know what is going on and what is coming up. In my office, we hold sales meetings to review the files and closings to ensure that all details are attended to and that our files are perfectly organized in our document and transaction management system.

KEY POINTS FROM CHAPTER 10:

1. Know what you are agreeing to before signing.

2. Ask questions when you don't understand terms in the contract.

3. Understand the ways the seller and the buyer can get out of the contract.

4. Buyers who write offers like your home, so try to make it work.

5. Take note of what you and your agent need to do to ensure a successful transaction.

CHAPTER 11

PACKING AND MOVING

If you apply the principles from this book, you are probably going to sell quickly. Below is a moving checklist and a list of packing tips, provided by Movers USA, to help you get on your way to your new home.

Moving Checklist

Two Months Prior to Moving:

There are so many things to think about when moving! Here's a comprehensive checklist to help you stay on track:

❑ Clean. Go through every room of your house and decide what you'd like to keep and what you can get rid of. Think about whether any items will require special packing or extra insurance coverage.

❏ Research. Start investigating moving company options. Do not rely on a quote over the phone; request an on-site estimate. Get an estimate in writing from each company, and make sure it has a USDOT (US Department of Transportation) number on it.

❏ Create a moving binder. Use this binder to keep track of everything—all your estimates, your receipts, and an inventory of all the items you're moving.

❏ Organize school records. Go to your children's school and arrange for their records to be transferred to their new school district.

Six Weeks Prior to Moving:

❏ Order supplies. Order boxes and other supplies such as tape, Bubble Wrap, and permanent markers. Don't forget to order specialty containers, such as dish barrels or wardrobe boxes.

❏ Start using up things that you don't want to move, like frozen or perishable foods and cleaning supplies.

❏ Take measurements. Check room dimensions at your new home, if possible, and make sure larger pieces of furniture will fit through the door.

One Month Prior to Moving:

☐ Choose your mover and confirm the arrangements. Select a company and get written confirmation of your moving date, costs, and other details.

☐ Begin packing. Start packing the things that you use most infrequently, such as the waffle iron and croquet set. While packing, note items of special value that might require additional insurance from your moving company. Make sure to declare, in writing, any items valued over one hundred dollars per pound, such as a computer.

☐ Label. Clearly label and number each box with its contents and the room it's destined for. This will help you to keep an inventory of your belongings. Pack and label "essentials" boxes of items you'll need right away.

☐ Separate valuables. Add items such as jewelry and important files to a safe box that you'll personally transport to your new home. Make sure to put the mover's estimate in this box. You'll need it for reference on moving day.

☐ Do a change of address. Go to your local post office and fill out a change-of-address form, or do it online at usps.gov. But in case there are stragglers, it's always wise to ask a close neighbor to look out for mail after you've moved. Check in with him or her two weeks after the move, and again two weeks after that.

☐ Notify important parties. Alert the following of your move: banks, brokerage firms, your

employer's human resources department, magazines and newspapers you subscribe to, and credit
card, insurance, and utility companies.

❑ Forward medical records. Arrange for medical
records to be sent to any new health-care pro-
viders or obtain copies of them yourself. Ask for
referrals.

Two Weeks Prior to Moving:

❑ Arrange to be off from work on moving day. Notify
your office that you plan to supervise the move and
therefore need the day off.

❑ Take your car to a garage, and ask the mechanic to
consider what services might be needed if you're
moving to a new climate.

❑ Clean out your safe-deposit box. If you'll be changing banks, remove the contents of your safe-deposit
box and put them in the safe box that you'll take
with you on moving day.

❑ Contact the moving company. Reconfirm the
arrangements.

One Week Prior to Moving:

❑ Refill prescriptions. Stock up on prescriptions you'll
need during the next couple of weeks.

❑ Pack your suitcases. Aim to finish your general
packing a few days before your moving date. Then
pack suitcases for everyone in the family with
enough clothes to wear for a few days.

A Few Days Prior to Moving:

❑ Defrost the freezer. If your refrigerator is moving with you, make sure to empty, clean, and defrost it at least twenty-four hours before moving day.

❑ Reconfirm the moving company's arrival time and other specifics and make sure you have prepared exact, written directions to your new home for the staff. Include contact information, such as your cell phone number.

❑ Plan for the payment. If you haven't already arranged to pay your mover with a credit card, get a money order, cashier's check, or cash for payment and tip.

Moving Day:

❑ Verify that the moving truck that shows up is from the company you hired: The USDOT number painted on its side should match the number on the estimate you were given.

❑ Take inventory. Before the movers leave, sign the bill of lading and/or inventory list and keep a copy.

———

Packing Tips

If you plan to do your own packing, the most important part is preplanning. Mistakes that may result in damages can be made when things are packed in a hurry. Some of these tips may seem like common sense, but they are often forgotten in the midst of a move.

- ❏ If you will be using boxes that you got from the grocery store, check them carefully for bugs.
- ❏ Begin by packing items you do not use every day.
- ❏ Label each box, indicating in which room it should go. Mark fragile boxes boldly so the movers will exercise extra care.
- ❏ Upholstered items should be covered with protective plastic to prevent stains or damage.
- ❏ Rugs and similar items should be cleaned before the move.
- ❏ Remove bulbs and shades from all lamps. Lampshades should be packed separately in a sturdy box. To protect your lampshades, wrap them in Bubble Wrap. Do not use newspaper as it may leave smudges.
- ❏ Valuables should be removed and kept with you. This includes legal documents, financial records, insurance policies, computer backup drives, jewelry, cash, and credit cards.
- ❏ Glass tabletops and glass doors on furniture should be crated with Bubble Wrap and heavy cardboard for safe shipping.
- ❏ Dry and canned foods may be shipped as long as they are packed in a sturdy box. Liquids should be discarded or thrown away.

❑ Chemical and hazardous materials such as but not limited to propane tanks, pool chemicals, fertilizers, paint thinners, solvents, bleach, aerosol cans, and firearms cannot be shipped. Lawn mowers and other equipment with gas tanks must be completely drained prior to shipping.

❑ Drawers in furniture should be cleared of liquid and heavy items. Only light clothing may be left in sturdy furniture.

❑ Appliances should be disconnected prior to your moving team arriving. Also, take down shelves, light fixtures, or chandeliers, if applicable.

❑ Items needing special handling such as pool tables, Jacuzzis, and grandfather clocks should be disassembled by a professional before moving day. Once these items have been disassembled, your movers can pack and ship them for you.

❑ Pack largest and heaviest items in the bottom of box first. Books and other heavy items should be packed in small boxes.

❑ Large mirrors or pictures should be wrapped individually, covering both sides with Bubble Wrap and heavy cardboard, and then binding with tape.

❑ Items should be packed in boxes that are the proper size. If there is empty space in the box, use wadded-up packing paper to fill up space.

❑ Small appliances and electronics should be packed in the boxes they came in whenever possible.

❑ For dishes and glassware, you should use specially designed dish packages. Pack dishes on their sides wrapped in newspaper or with packing paper in between them.

❏ If you disassemble any furniture yourself, remember to put the hardware in a plastic bag and attach it with tape so it will not be lost.

❏ Wrap sharp tools to prevent injury.

❏ Computers and printers should be wrapped in plastic bags first, and then packed in the box they came in or a similar sturdy box. Check the owner's manual for tips in securing internal components. Repack those boxes in a second, individual box. Fill empty space with Bubble Wrap or cardboard. Remove printer cartridge. Mark "Fragile" and "This End Up" and the room destination.

❏ Stereos, CD players, VCRs, and DVDs should be wrapped in plastic bags and then in the original cartons or similar sturdy boxes. Check the owner's manual for additional packing tips. Repack those boxes in a second, individual box. Mark "Fragile" and "This End Up" and the room destination.

❏ We recommend that clothing be packed in wardrobe boxes. Depending on the size of the garment, these boxes can hold up to twenty-five hangers. Fill the bottom of the boxes with shoes or other lightweight items.

Reprinted with permission from Movers USA, http://www.1movers.com. You may also be interested in a "List of things to do" prior to moving: http://www.1movers.com/resources/tips/info/list-of-things-to-do/.

KEY POINTS FROM CHAPTER 11:

1. Ask your agent for mover recommendations.

2. Start interviewing movers at least two months in advance.

3. Hire reputable, highly recommended movers.

4. Be familiar with all the items you own and consider the best way to pack them safely and securely.

5. Planning and preparation are key.

CONCLUSION

As you can see from the thought, substance, and expertise packed into this book, it isn't an easy or simple task to list and sell your home. However, there is definitively a right way to get it done. I hope you have learned the value of hiring a truly competent professional who understands what it really takes to sell your home and will be honest with you about the selling process.

My style is very candid, truthful, and supportive, so this book has been designed for the client who can handle the unfiltered truth. As a business owner, I strive to sensitively deliver honesty supported by facts, data, and logic. Clients appreciate the research and thoughtfulness of my approach. I believe in my heart it is the right way to do business.

My parting words: it will cost you more to work with a novice than it does to work with an experienced, successful professional!

ABOUT THE AUTHOR

Raised in Anne Arundel County, Maryland, David Orso attended Severna Park High School and grew up playing golf, lacrosse, and basketball. He attended the University of Dayton on a golf scholarship and earned a bachelor's degree in psychology. He continued his studies at Loyola College, earning an MBA with a concentration in strategic marketing.

David found a passion for residential real estate when he started buying rental properties in 2001. With over thirteen years in real estate, David has managed well over 1000 residential transactions and volume greater than $500 million. He currently works as an agent affiliated with Century 21 New Millennium, the number one Century 21 firm in the world. David is ranked number one in Maryland within his firm and number eighteen in the entire United States for all of Century 21, as of July 2014. He was voted the number one real estate agent by the readers of the *Severna Park Voice*, a local newspaper in his area. David was also named one of REAL Trends' Best Real Estate Agents in America.

David is active in his community, including serving on the Building Traditions Society's Board of Directors and the Pediatric Council at Anne Arundel Medical Center.

He also volunteers as a coach for the local Broadneck area youth sports program. In 2002, he helped start a nonprofit program in Baltimore that introduced underprivileged youth to the game of golf. David was selected to be on the Board of Directors for Chartwell Golf and Country Club through 2016. David is married with three children and currently resides in Arnold, Maryland.